All precious flowers in the garden of wisdom
come from the Infinite Source.
This book is dedicated with heartfelt gratitude to
Her Holiness Shri Mataji Nirmala Devi.

Book has been compiled by Sona Agarwal. Special thanks for their contribution goes to Herbert Reininger, Sowmya Rajeshkumar, Monika Shinde, Nikhil Agarwal. Proofreading done by Flurina Wollenberger, Rama Godavarthi, Victoria Zbylut, and Saumya Nageet.

Illustrations made by the following artists:
Agarwal Sona - pages 11, 12, 63, 57
Dallosova Jana - pages 19, 32, 41, 47
Denisova Ekaterina - page 4
Fusseli Vijaya - page 23
Ghosh Shanti - page 35
Ghosh Saumya - page 5
Pearce Tejas & Aria - page 60
Tischuk Eliska - pages 7, 28, 30
Maria Martinez - pages 52, 60, 61

Adi Guru Dattatreya is the prototype or original model from which all gurus emerge. He is the Guru Principle. As the Adi Guru, He has incarnated many times to guide mankind. He came as the ten great Primordial Masters, from Janaka through to Sai Nath. This great principle has incarnated to give from to God's love for mankind, returning again and again to correct our mistakes and bring us back to a God-centered life. Lord Dattatreya himself is the essence and innocence of Shri Brahmadeva, Shri Vishnu and Shri Shiva. He is the integration of all the three Gunas, and above all is innocense itself.

"You can say the Mediterranean Sea, that is void, where all this activity took

place. This activity took place because there were ten main, these great prophets, were born. And these prophets are the people who are made out of the innocence, the innocence of these three aspects of Him (Adi Guru).
The innocence of these three aspects of God is made into a personality called Dattatreya or the Primordial Master.

Dattatreya He comes on this earth again and again. Specially ten are the main, main incarnations. So He comes again and again on this earth to tell people about their dharma, their religion, their capacity, their quality."[1]

Raja Janaka

Raja Janaka was the king of Mithila, India sometime between 16,000 BC. and 10,000 BC. He was an enlightened person, teaching detachment in all circumstances, pure attention based on dharma (inner religion and moral behavior) and the Spirit. Raja Janaka is revered as an ideal example of detachment to material possessions. As a king, he had access to luxuries and pleasures far beyond the ordinary, but his internal state was close to that of a sadhu (holy man). He was intensely interested in spiritual discourse and considered himself free from worldly illusions. Raja Janaka was the first of the ten primordial masters who incarnated. He was the father of Shri Sita who represents the feminine aspect of the Divine principle and the source of strength for the Right Heart Chakra.

Birth Of Sita

King Janaka and his wife Sunayana did not have any children, they prayed to God to bless them with a child. One day when king Janaka was ploughing a field to perform a yagna (religious ceremony), he found the plough stuck in the field. No amount of effort would make it move. The earth around the plough was cleared away, and suddenly, a box with a beautiful baby girl appeared at that spot! Raja Janaka was amazed at this miracle and was overjoyed since he did not have a daughter of his own. He placed her affectionately on his lap and overwhelmed with love, he declared her as his own child. The baby was the daughter of Bhumi Devi, Goddess of the Earth. The tip of the plough is called Sita in Sanskrit and therefore the baby was named Sita. She was also known as Janaki, as the daughter of king Janaka. Sunayana and king Janaka raised Sita with lots of tender care and love. King Janaka was a very religious and spiritually inclined man. He was always surrounded by wise, learned sages and Rishis. There were often long debates at his court on matters of religion, spirituality and inner development.

As Janaka was inclined to seek inner solace rather than outwardly bodily pleasures he was called Videh, detached from the physical matter.

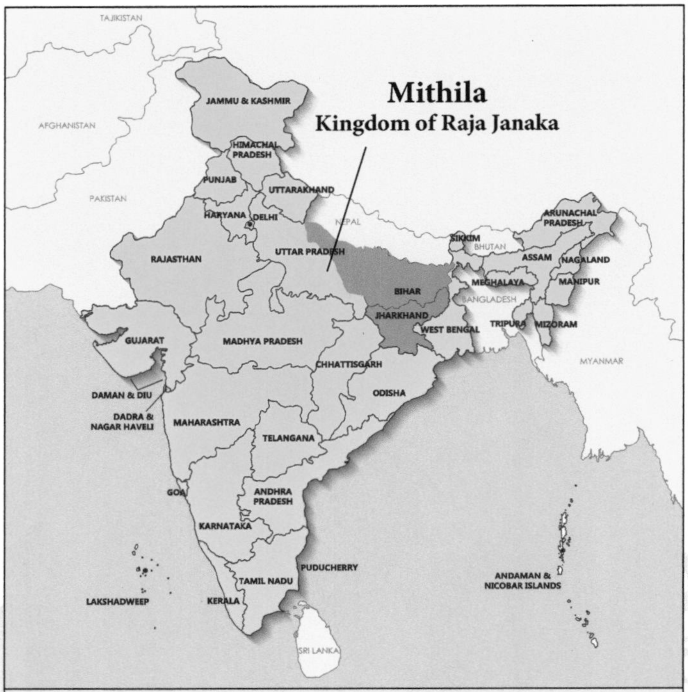

Where is Mithila today?

"The majority of Mithila region falls within modern-day India, more specifically in the state of Bihar. Mithila is bounded in the North by the Himalayas, and in the South, West and East by the rivers Ganges, Gandaki and Mahananda respectively. It extends into the Southeastern Terai of Nepal."[2]

Shri Mataji On Raja Janaka

"What are the powers of the right side, now, which are achieved through the left-side perfection? We have some very great Gurus on this line. One of them was Raja Janaka. He was a ruler of a country, and a very well-known ruler and everything; but still, still, though He was so generous and good and everything, but at the same time he was a great monarch, great king of those days, very much known for his impartiality, for his statesmanship and all kinds of beautiful things he did for his subjects. He could not get disturbed with anything. And people never understood why the greatest of greatest saints used to bow to him. What was so great? Though he was a king, he was living so lavishly, and he had so many ornaments and also conveyances and all that; because nothing was above him, he was so detached with everything. He had everything, but he was so detached. That's a very good example of a person who had mastered his left side."[3]

Nachiketa Gets Angry

"King Janaka was called as Bidehi - means an ascetic. And he was a king and whenever he went to any ashram the saints used to get up and touch his feet. So, one disciple of a guru got very angry. His name was Nachiketa and he said, "How can you all touch his feet when he is a king and enjoying life like a king, living like a king, wearing a crown? How can you touch his feet?" So, the guru said. "He is the primordial master. To him it does not matter whether he lives in a palace or on the street."[4]

Bowl Of Milk Story

"Great sage Narada asked him (Raja Janaka) one day, 'Revered Sir, how are you called as Bideha, you live in this world, how can you be a Bidehi? 'Raja Janaka said, 'This is very simple. I will tell you about it in the evening. Now, please do this little job for me. There is milk in this bowl. You take this bowl and come along with me. Please see that not a single drop of milk is spilled on the Earth. Then only I will tell you why I am called Bidehi'. Narada took the bowl and followed Janaka everywhere. He had to be very careful because the bowl was such

Janaka was so detached with everything. He had everything, but He was so detached. That's very good example of a person who had mastered His left side.

that by the slightest movement the milk might have spilled. He got very tired. When they returned in the evening, Narada asked, 'Please tell me now, I am quite fed up with carrying this bowl and following you everywhere at the same time. 'Raja Janaka said, 'First of all tell me what you have seen?' Narada, 'Nothing except this bowl of milk so that it won't spill.' Raja Janaka, 'Didn't you see, there was a big procession in my honor, then there was a court wherein there was program of dancing? Didn't you see anything? 'Narada said, 'No sir, I have not seen anything. 'Raja Janaka, 'My child, likewise with me, I also see nothing. All the time, I just watch my attention, where is it going? Making sure that it won't spill away like the milk.' "This sort of attention one has to develop: chitta nirodh. Nirodh means the saving of your attention, so your attention should not be on saving money and worldly things and all that, but attention itself must be saved. As you watch your money, as you watch your road when you drive, as you watch

> "I can give you all my kingdom but not Self-Realization, very difficult because you are possessed by the idea of money, such a person cannot get Realization."

your child, when it is growing, as you watch the beauty of your wife, or the care of your husband, all put together you watch your self – your attention."[5]

Burning Palace Story

"Next day, he (Nachiketa) went to Raja Janaka and asked him, 'Give me Self-Realization.' So, Raja Janaka said, 'I can give you all my kingdom but not Self-realization, very difficult because you are possessed by the idea of money, such a person cannot get Realization.' He said, 'All right, I will live here till I get Realization.' Next day Raja Janaka took him for a bath in the river and he was enjoying the bath. And people came and told him that there is a fire in his palace. But Raja Janaka was meditating, he didn't bother. Then they said that the people who are in the palace have run away. Then he says that somebody said that now the fire is coming here. Still, Raja Janaka was meditating. But Nachiketa ran out because his clothes were outside, so ran out to save himself... and still Raja Janaka was not bothered. So, when he (Raja Janaka) came out (of meditation) he told Nachiketa, 'Nachiketa, this is all Mahamaya.' This is how you are tested, if you are money-oriented you cannot get Self-realization. She (Kundalini) is the one who is testing you.

So, the first thing you must have is satisfaction. This is a very important thing in modern times to understand. You work very hard, save money to buy a carpet, then you have the carpet, you want to have a house - you never enjoy the carpet. Then you have a house, so when you get the house, you want to have a car, then from a car, you want, I think, helicopter, maybe an airplane. Because of this, in these modern times, people are extremely restless, but if you have this Lakshmi Principle in you, you will feel extremely satisfied with everything that is materialistic."[6]

Why Do We Need A Guru

"The word Guru comes from the one that is magnetic, the person who is magnetic, the one who attracts the attention of the seekers, is the Guru. Also, it means the heaviness, or you can say, a person who is very steady, who is very deep, who has the knowledge, and who can act like the Mother Earth. For the power of magnetism in the Mother Earth also is called as magnetic, but in Sanskrit is 'Gurutwakareshwari'– which means the attraction of the heaviness of the Mother Earth. But actually, it is a power of the Mother Earth that makes us stand properly on our legs when it is rotating with such a tremendous speed, otherwise we would be all thrown away. With that velocity that she is moving, we are still attached, or we are one in our balance, this is only because she has gravity. This gravity has to be in a Guru. Gravity means a kind of a serious understanding of oneself and one's own responsibilities. So, a Guru has to be very steady."[7]

"Now, it is important that we have to establish the dharma within us.

Without the dharma you cannot have the ascent.

And as I have told you before that the cleanliness of your being depends on how much dharma you follow, religiously.

Questions & Answers

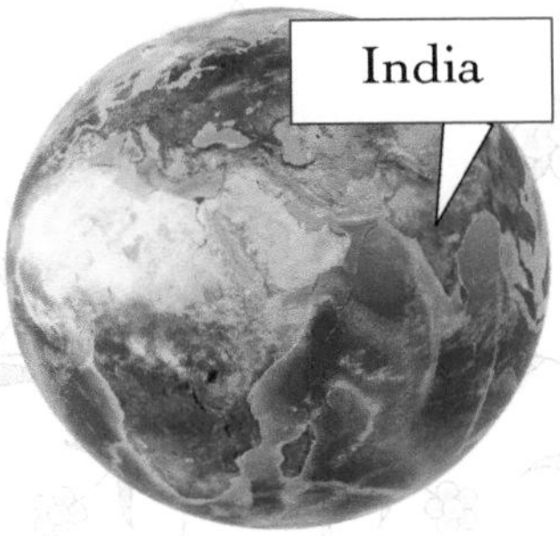

When and where was Raja Janaka born?
- Raja Janaka was born sometime between 16,000 and 10,000 BC in Mithila, India.

Describe what type of a king was Raja Janaka.
- He was a king who was not attached to material possessions. He was generous, and good to everyone.

Raja Janaka had his left side under complete control. How did having strong left side show in his life?
- Raja Janaka was completely detached. Detachment is a quality of the left side.

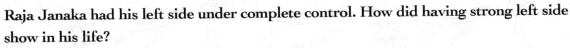

Raja Janaka found his daughter Sita. Where did he find her?
- Raja Janaka found Sita in Mother Earth while ploughing.

What was Raja Janaka doing when he was told that his palace was on fire? What was his reaction?
- Raja Janaka was meditating by river. His reaction was no reactio because he was detached from the material world.

ABRAHAM

The story of Abraham is the story of a man, on an amazing journey who, travelled for 40 years. It is a journey of faith, hardship, sacrifice, disappointment and of great reward!

Qualities As Guru

His life was a clear demonstration of complete faith and surrender to God`s will. Over 4,000 years ago, he was called to begin a wonderful journey. Even under the most unbelievable circumstances or requests, he was ready to fully trust and follow the Divine. Several times he abandoned his land, home and livelihood which he had made for himself and for his family. He then had to start afresh over and over again. Many times, when Lord told him to, he had to let go of his closest and most beloved family members.

Though always seeking peace and avoiding the troubles, Abraham had the courage to fight when he had to protect his family or friends that were taken prisoners; he manifested amazing compassion and perfect fairness when he dealt with war prisoners.

Childhood

Abraham was born and brought up in the magnificent city of Iraq, during the Ur civilization, around 2,000 BC. His family left Ur, present day Iraq, to travel Northwest along the Euphrates River to the city of Haran. Abraham settled down in Haran, in modern day Israel, with his family. At the time, Haran as well as all the neighboring cities and countries, was a land devoted to polytheism (worship of more than one god).

Journey Begins

When Abraham was in Haran, at the age of 75, he got the call from God to leave his home and

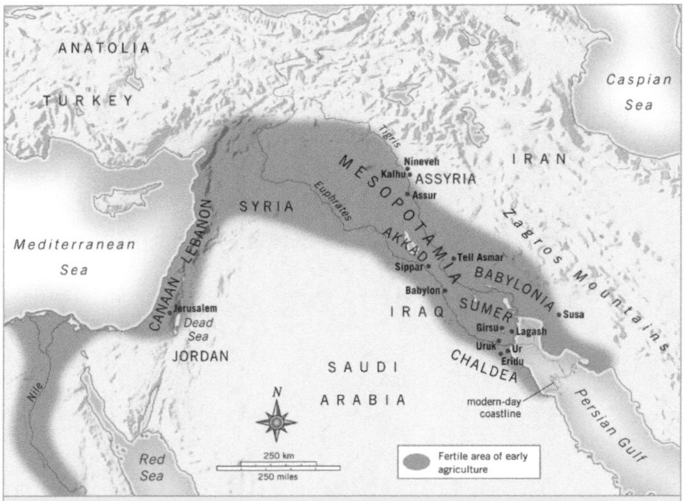

"Mesopotamia is a region of southwest Asia in the Tigris and Euphrates river system that benefitted from the area's climate and geography to host the beginnings of human civilization (Middle East today)."[8]

family behind. He was to follow God into a strange land that God would give him. So, Abraham moved with his wife, Sarai, and his nephew, Lot, towards the promised land Canaan, located in the pres-

"Mother Kundalini please awaken within me the powers and the guru qualities of Shri Abraham. Please, give me the power of faith of complete surrender and moral strength that Shri Abraham has, so I can be a pure and strong Guru."

TURKEY
Haran
TigrisRiver
Euphrates River
Damascus
MEDITERRANEAN
SEA
CANAAN
SYRIA
Mari
Babylon
Zoan
HEBRON
UR
Mount
SINAI
LIBYA
SAUDI
ARABIA
EGYPT
Nile River
RED
SEA
SUDAN
ETHIOPIA

His life is a clear demonstration of complete faith and surrender to God's will, even under the most unbelievable circumstances or requests he was ready to absolutely trust and follow the divine.

ent-day Israel. As a period of famine came, he and his wife went down to Egypt where they lived for some years and then returned to Canaan. Abram took his wife, his nephew, Lot, and his possessions and departed. Abraham moved South into the land of Canaan which was inhabited by the warrior people called Canaanites. He settled temporarily in Shechem and Bethel.

A famine in the land forced Abraham and his people to move to Egypt. Fearful that Pharaoh would kill Abraham for his beautiful wife, Abraham asked Sarai, his wife, to pretend to be his sister instead. Pharaoh noted Sarai and took her away from Abraham. For this, he was struck with a plague. When Pharaoh got to know Sarai's true identity, he was angry with Abraham. He returned Sarai and asked them to leave Egypt. Abraham left Egypt with carts of wealth.

Starting from Ur, Abraham traveled 700 miles to the borders of present-day Iraq, then another 700 miles into Syria, then another 800 down to Egypt, and then back into Canaan. Abraham died when he was 175 years old.

Sacrificing Abraham`s Son

Later, the faith of Abraham was tested by God, as He, the Almighty, asked Abraham to sacrifice his most beloved son Isaac. The devoted Abraham made up an altar and was about to kill his son, when an Angel of God stopped him as he passed this ultimate test of faith.

One God, No Idol Story

Abraham's father, Terach was an idol-manufacturer. Once he had to travel, so he left Abraham to manage the shop. People would come in and ask to buy idols. Abraham would say, "How old are you?" The person would say, "Fifty," or "Sixty". Abraham would say, "Isn't it pathetic that a man of sixty wants to bow down to a one-day-old idol?" The man would feel ashamed and leave.

One time a woman came with a basket of bread. She said to Abraham, "Take this and offer it to the gods". Abraham got up, took a hammer in his hand, broke all the idols to pieces, and then put the hammer in the hand of the biggest idol among them.

When his father came back and saw the broken idols, he was appalled. "Who did this?" he cried. "How can I hide anything from you?" replied Abraham calmly. "A woman came with a basket of bread and told me to offer it to them. I brought it in front of them, and each one said, "I'm going to eat first." Then the biggest one got up, took the hammer and broke all the others to pieces."

"What are you trying to pull on me?" asked Terach, "Do they have minds?"Said Abraham: "Listen to what your own mouth is saying? They have no power at all! Why worship idols?"

Abraham's Journey from Ur to Canaan with his family.

Shri Mataji On Abraham

"Abraham had problems of talking to people who were really very, very ignorant.
He didn't know what to do with them. So only, you can see it, in the time of Abraham that His own lifestyle… I mean, that was just a system when the family was building up and the relationships were building up, and He tried to work it on that level. Now Abraham and Moses are, all these Primordial Masters that are concerned with your attention and with your sustenance. So, all of them, whether it was Mohammed or anyone, have talked against alcohol, you see. It was their job was to look after the sustenance of the stomach and we can see clearly, that how can anybody who is of Christ's quality, give you wine to drink, which goes against your awareness. It is impossible...
Even you'll be surprised that Abraham or Moses did not talk of spirituality. They talked of God, but not of spirituality. "[9]

Wine Is Grape Juice

"Oh, you see that's another big mistake. That time wine was not this kind of a wine. You see people used to take wine which is grape juice. Even today if you go to Jerusalem, you get wine which is not fermented. It is prohibited, in the Bible if you read Moses or Abraham, to take these strong drinks, it is described very clearly. There's a difference between wine and alcohol, wine which is fermented and wine which is a real wine. You see otherwise He would have said fermented wine. And, that's a very common drink and I also enjoy it very much, grapes I love."[10]

Recognize Yourself

"Abraham – how many people recognized him? He was never recognized, never understood, that was the problem, and this is what one has to understand. The time has come now to recognize, to understand. Recognize yourself that you are the Spirit – not this body, not this mind, not this ego - nothing - but you are the Spirit."[11]

Questions & Answers

When and where was Abraham born?
- He was born in Ur, Iraq, 2,000 BC

How many years did Abraham spend travelling before settling down?
- Abraham spent 40 years travelling.

Name three things we can learn from Abraham.
- Obedience to God, faith in God and one God worship (the true God worship).

Why did Abraham break idols in his father's shop?
- Because Abraham thought that idol statues have no power and therefore there was no need to worship them.

Why did God ask Abraham to sacrifice his son Isaac?
- God wanted to test faith and surrender of Abraham in him.

MOSES

Pharaoh Ramses II was an Egyptian ruler (1304-1237 BC) who ordered all the baby boys to be killed at birth out of fear that the Hebrew slaves were becoming greater in number. Moses' mother hid her son until she could no longer keep him safe.So, she placed baby Moses in a basket and let the basket drift on the Nile River. He was rescued by the pharaoh's daughter who raised him like her son. Moses grew up as an Egyptian prince, even though he knew he was a Hebrew. Hebrews were slaves in Egypt at that time. One day, Moses was out walking and saw an Egyptian

Moses was a prophet who lead the Israelites out of slavery in Egypt across the Red Sea to Canaan. Present day Lebanon, Syria, Jordan, and Israel.

man insulting a Hebrew man. Moses wanted to help a fellow Israelite and in doing so, he ended up hurting the Egyptian man. When the pharaoh heard what Moses had done, he was angry. "Moses will be punished," he said. Out of fear, Moses ran away into the desert. He ran for a long time, but then, he reached a place where he found a well. There, he saw some young women fetching water for their sheep. A group of shepherds tried to drive them away. Moses helped the women and their sheep by driving away the shepherds. The father of those women was grateful and gave Moses a job as well as one of his daughters in marriage.

The Burning Bush Story

Many years passed, and Moses worked tending sheep for his father-in-law. One day, he was watching his sheep when he spotted something unusual. It was a bush that was on fire, but it didn't burn to the ground. Moses knew that a bush

God speaking to Moses through the burning bush.

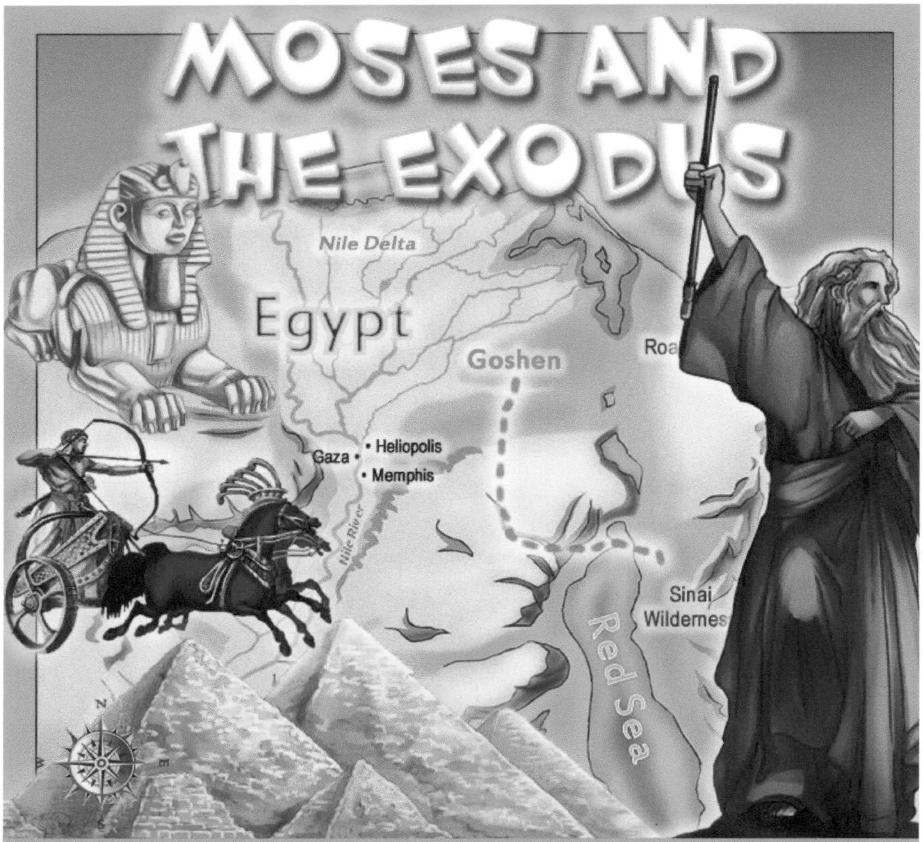

A map of the Israeli exodus, led by Moses. They journeyed from Egypt to the promised land of freedom.

on fire should burn up. "What a strange sight," he said. "I must take a closer look." He turned toward the burning bush. "Moses! Moses!" The voice came from the burning bush! Do bushes talk? Moses was thinking to himself.

"Remove your sandals. This place is holy. I am thy God." Said the Voice. Moses was afraid and hid his face. God said to him "The Egyptians have mistreated my people, the Israelites. I have heard them crying and asking me for help. I will free them and send them to a good land. You will go to the pharaoh and tell him to set my people free." Moses was filled with doubt and asked God, "Who am I to do this?" At first, Moses did not want to obey and said that he was not good with words, but when he was told that his brother Aaron would go to Egypt with him, Moses agreed.

Moses And The Pharaoh

When Moses and his brother Aaron reached Egypt, the Lord told them what to do. He said, "Go to Pharaoh and tell him to let the Israelites go. He will be very stubborn and won't listen. It will take many signs and miracles before he will let you go. Everyone will know that I am God when he finally will let the Israelites go." As a self-proclaimed God in human form, Ramses was not accustomed to take orders from lesser Gods, let alone an unknown God like Yahweh (God of the kingdom of Israel). "Who is the Lord," Ramses inquired, "that I should heed his voice and let the Israelites go? I do not know the Lord, and moreover I will not let Israelites go." Thus, the stage was set for a long struggle between a distrustful ruler with an outsized ego and the prophet Moses, who had a new understanding of the power of Yahweh. One day, God asked Moses and Aaron to go see the pharaoh. In front of Pharaoh, Moses threw down his staff, and it became a snake, just as God had told him. Pharaoh didn't look surprised at all, he actually just smiled at Moses. Without a word, he snapped his fingers and a minute later, three men walked in. Pharaoh whispered in one of the men's ears, and the man nodded. The man then spoke quietly to the others. All at the same time, the men threw their staffs on the ground which turned into snakes, just like Moses. At that moment, Moses realized that these men were the pharaoh's magicians.

"Nice try, but the Israelites belong to me, and they work for Egypt. I will not let them go," said Pharaoh.

Moses met Pharaoh the next morning again and explained to him, "Because you still won't listen and free my people, the water of the Nile is going to change into blood. The fish will die, the river will stink, and none of the Egyptians will be able to drink its water."

The pharaoh smiled and said, "Go ahead." So, Moses did what The Lord had told him. He put his staff into the water, and it turned into blood. Pharaoh seemed a little surprised, but he summoned his magicians, and they turned more of the water into blood. With that, the pharaoh's heart became hard, and he walked away, back to his palace. After a whole week of this, Pharaoh still wouldn't let the people go, but neither could his magicians turn the blood back into water.

The Lord instructed Moses to go see Pharaoh once again. God said, "Tell Pharaoh to let my people go. If he refuses to let them go, I will plague the whole country with frogs." After a day of this, the pharaoh couldn't take it anymore, and he called for Moses. He begged Moses, "Pray to your Lord to take the frogs away from me and my people, then I will let your people go." So, Moses prayed to the Lord, and all the frogs died. But when Pharaoh saw that all the frogs were dead, he was relieved, but his heart hardened again, so he changed his mind. There were many other plagues that followed: Gnats and flies, then all the livestock died of sickness. The Egyptians were covered

10 Plagues of Egypt

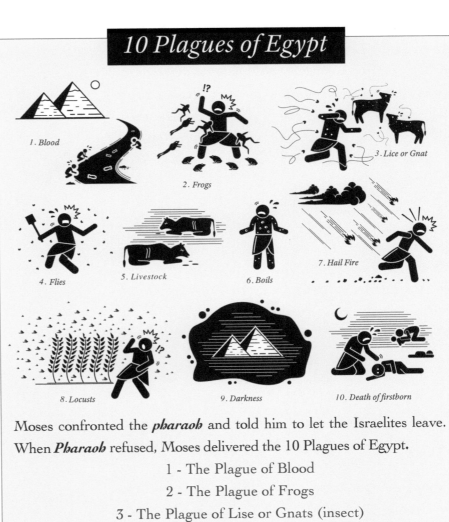

Moses confronted the ***pharaoh*** and told him to let the Israelites leave. When ***Pharaoh*** refused, Moses delivered the 10 Plagues of Egypt.

1 - The Plague of Blood

2 - The Plague of Frogs

3 - The Plague of Lise or Gnats (insect)

4 - The Plague of Flies

5 - The Plague on Livestock

6 - The Plague of Boils

7 - The Plague of Hail

8 - The Plague of Locusts

9 - The Plague of Darkness

10- The Plague on the Firstborn

Moses gave us the balancing, and he gave us the so-called, we can say the religion as we call it, dharma. The one by which you sustain yourself.

in sores, then hail came down that damaged their crops. Locusts came and ate all the grass, as well as anything green. Then, there was complete darkness which forced people to not leave their homes as they couldn't see anything.

With each of these plagues, Pharaoh said he would let the Israelites go if God put things back to normal, but like before, he would always change his mind. God sent one more plague (the tenth plague) that was far worse than any of the previous ones. The Lord said, "This will be the last plague on Pharaoh and Egypt, after this he will let you go. Around midnight, I will go throughout all of Egypt, and every firstborn son or animal in Egypt will die, even the son of the pharaoh, and there will be great sadness." Moses warned the pharaoh, who refused to listen. After midnight, Pharaoh realized what was happening in Egypt and summoned for Moses. He said to Moses, "Leave my people. You and all the Israelites are to leave Egypt immediately!

The pharaoh finally decided to let the Israelites go and they migrated in large numbers from Egypt. The pharaoh later changed his mind and followed Moses and his people with an army to attack them.

In order to save his people, Moses made the Red Sea part and make way for the Israelites to pass. The Israelites were safe, but the pharaoh's army, when they tried to cross the sea in pursuit, were destroyed. Moses led the Israelites through the wilderness and God helped them along the way by providing manna (type of grain), quails to eat, and water from the rocks to drink. When Moses came to Mount Sinai, he went up on the mountain to receive the Ten Commandments and other laws from God.

Fun Facts

• Moses took the Israelites across the Red Sea, parting the waters as the people made an exodus (a mass departure of people) from Egypt. After that, he led them through forty years of wandering through the wilderness.

• He lived to be 120 years old. His long and varied life can be divided into three parts, each 40 years long. The first, as the son of an Egyptian pharaoh, the second, as a shepherd, and the third, as the esteemed leader of Israel.

• During their wandering through the wilderness, they camped for two years at Mount Sinai. There, Moses was given the laws to be observed in the Promised Land.

Mount Sinai - Moses spent 40 days on the top of the mountain talking to God. When he came down he brought the Ten Commandments down to teach to the Israelites, but they had made idols instead of God who brought them out of slavery.

The 10 Commandments

God gave Moses the Ten Commandments on Mount Sinai to serve as principles of moral behavior for the human race. The Ten Commandments of God are the foundation of the moral code and legal system of justice.

1. **You shall have no other gods before me.**
2. **You shall not make for yourselves an idol.**
3. **You shall not misuse the name of the Lord, your God.**
4. **Remember the Sabbath day by keeping it holy.**
5. **Honor your father and your mother.**
6. **You shall not murder.**
7. **You shall not commit adultery.**
8. **You shall not steal.**
9. **You shall not give false testimony.**
10. **You shall not covet (having no lust).**

The Ten Commandments were written by God on two stone tablets. God also told Moses the instructions of a priests' duties. Moses was on the mountain for forty days and forty nights. Meanwhile, the people were waiting for Moses and did not find him. They made Aaron, his brother, make a calf out of gold and worshiped it. God warned Moses about it. When Moses came down and saw what they had done, he was very angry with them. The people of the Levi tribes forgot all about the God who led them out of Egypt. Instead, they began an idol worship.

Shri Mataji On Moses

"Why did Moses talk of the balance? Why did He talk of the Ten Commandments? For what? I mean, every intelligent man must ask. Every Jew must ask, "For what?" Because without balance you cannot ascend. I mean, even an airplane has to be a balanced thing to ascend. Anything, I mean, we have to have a balance. So, to establish the balance within us, these people came again and again, these ten primordial beings, we say. Some of them on the left-hand side, some on the right-hand side. It's so wonderful. So, now we can say who they were

Moses crossed the ocean by creating a path. That's one of the very significant things which shows that the Void can be crossed with the help of the Guru.

from the very beginning, very symbolic. First of all, they were against alcohol, against any kind of intoxication. But say, at the time of Moses, they didn't have cigarettes, you see, so He didn't say about cigarettes. So, the people who follow Moses think there's nothing wrong with cigarettes because He didn't say. But that time there were no cigarettes, you see."[12]

"Abraham had problems talking to people who were really very, very ignorant, and Moses had problems with people who were very indulgent people, so He had to pass the laws of Sharia. Moses passed the laws of Sharia, and if you read the Bible, in the first verse... Moses had to pass these laws, different, different laws to make the people follow religion precisely. So, He did not argue, He did not say, why you should do it, didn't give any explanation. "You do it!" Like that. Because He thought that these people are so ignorant that you cannot leave it to their freedom that you understand this or that you see the point; He could not do it that way. So He just said, "Alright. These are the laws, these are the things, and you have to follow. " Moses came on this earth to lay down the code of conduct, morality, the moral thing, and also He describes Milton as a person who describes a deity who is above everything, a puritanical deity. He describes the divine humanity. Also, He described the Christ, who came on this earth for the emancipation of human beings, not to tell them: "Don't do this and don't do that." That was all right at the time of Moses, in the beginning of it, the code of it, and He calls it a 'moral' Christianity, meaning 'immoral' must be, because if you force someone into something and pass such laws and regulations at this time, modern times, it's going to be impossible for human beings to follow, and they'll fall into some other traps."[13]

Prophets Have Special Qualities

"The prophets have special qualities, all the prophets had: First of all, they have to talk about spiritual education. All of them did that. Muhammad Sahib did it, Raja Janaka did it, Nanaka did it, Moses did it, Abraham did it. All of them prophesied and taught you how to lead yourself in the right path, by the right action, by leading a righteous life. These (Gurus) had great powers over oceans and over water. Like Moses – he crossed the ocean by creating a road. That's one of the very significant things which shows that the Void can be crossed with the help of the Guru.

...Now, another thing about these gurus: all these incarnations had to deal with your attention. So, they were particular about looking after your attention. And that is why, from the time Moses or Abraham came in, they talked of no alcoholism. All of them. It is written very clearly in the Bible that the strong alcohols, fermented, should not be taken."[14]

"So, the understanding of Mother Earth about saints is very great. She knows who the saint is, She knows the feet of a saint and that's why - you know so many things were created - like Moses. He went to the sea and the Mother Earth came up for them to walk through. If all the Jews had walked, it would not have worked, but it was Moses and His saintliness that the Mother Earth Herself came up and helped."[15]

Sharia Law

Sharia (meaning "the right path") regulates public and private behavior, and even private beliefs. Compared to other legal codes, the Sharia law also prioritizes punishment over rehabilitation and favors corporal and capital punishment over imprisonment."[16]

"In Egypt, because of the kings of those countries, who were very much interested in death, in their... what you call... graves, in building pyramids, all such things, not building up inside the dharma. This is a reason why in Egypt also the dharma went

Now, all these great incarnations had a special power over water. Because you know, in the stomach we have our Void and Nabhi chakra which are made of water. The ocean represents the incarnation of Adi Guru Dattatreya.

down very much and ultimately.

... In Peshawar these things happened, so it was very close also to Egypt and to Greece. But they became very much against Vishnu, because they thought their king was killed by them and all that. So, all these rakshasas entered into the area in Afghanistan and then they came to Egypt and to Greece, and tried to bring all the gods and goddesses to the ground. Long time back, must be at least ten thousand years back, when Prahalada brought in the incarnation of Shri Vishnu. These rakshasas went into their... called as asuras, Assyrians they call, but asuras they were. And if you go to Egypt, you'll find the Sphinx there. Just the opposite of what Narasimha was. The man is in the upper part and the lion is in the lower part.

But Narasimha is just the opposite. Narasimha is the lion in the upper part and the man in the lower part. So, they created this kind of an image which was just the o pposite of Vishnu. Because, just to show that we have another kind of a big incarnation, which is just the opposite and can fight Vishnu very well."[17]

Questions & Answers

When and where was Moses born? How old was Moses when he died?
- He was born in Egypt. He was 120 Years old when he died.

Why did Moses talk of the Ten Commandments?
- Moses talked of The Ten Commandments because it was a set of rules by which people should live and follow in order to ascend.

What did Moses bring back to the Israelites from Mount Sinai?
- He brought two tablets with the 10 Commandments.

Moses parted and crossed the ocean. This event was very significant to Sahaja Yogi/Yoginis. What is the significance of this event?
- The ocean represents the Void. Moses was the Adi Guru who lead people safely on the other side of the ocean. Meaning, that Moses wanted to show people that with the help of the guru, the Void can be crossed.

Why did Moses talk of balance?
- Moses talked of balance, because without balance one cannot ascend.

ZARATHUSTRA

Zarathustra was the 4th Adi Guru who incarnated on earth to help human beings cross "Bhav Sagara" or the Void. He is the incarnation of Lord "Shri Dattatreya" and was born in 630 BC. In the Zoroastrian system, wisdom is necessary for knowledge and knowledge is necessary for harmony with nature. Harmony with nature leads to righteousness and love, which leads to self-realization. Zarathustra described the seven qualities of the One and only God, Ahura Mazda. Not merely to make a compromise with the old religion of many deities, but he wanted his followers to strive to awaken these qualities in themselves.

Seven Qualities Of Ahura Mazda

1 - All knowing
2 - All powerful
3 - The creator of life
4 - The source of all goodness
5 - Impossible for humans to conceive
6 - Being everywhere (omnipresent)
7 - Unchanging

Creation was categorized in terms of seven elements – earth, sky, water, fire, plants, animals, and humans. Humans were under the guardianship of Ahura Mazda himself.

Zarathustra retreated to the mountains early in life to find answers to several spiritual issues. It is said that the Ahura Mazda himself revealed to Zarathustra the truths which he later taught among the people who accepted his teachings. "The Gathas", five in number, are the celestial songs intact in the words of Zarathustra himself, and they form the core of the religion. They are composed in 'Avesta' language which is extinct today and is a sister language of Sanskrit.

Raised index finger indicates there is only one God.

Zarathustra's Parents

Before the birth of Zarathustra, the magicians and wicked people knew that a person who would teach the people the true worship of Ahura Mazda was to be born to Dughdova (Zarathustra's mother). Ahura Mazda is the God Almighty.

Ahura is the male aspect, the Sadashiv. Mazda is the feminine aspect, the Adi Shakti. They wanted to kill her so that the people would not turn to Zarathustra for help from their wickedness. They told Frahimurva, the father of Dughdova, to let them kill her. Fearing for his daughter's life, her father sent her to live at the house of a friend Paitarasp, who lived in Persia. Paitarasp had a son whose name was Pourushaspa. Dughdova married Pourushaspa and they became the parents of Zarathustra.

Zarathustra's Birth Story

Zarathustra's birth was a very special event. Most babies cry at birth, but baby Zarathustra laughed at birth instead. This was an indication of the birth of a divine person.

Soon after his birth, an evil man named Durasarun planned to kill baby Zarathustra. He had heard that Zarathustra was sent by Ahura Mazda to get rid of evil.

To get rid of the baby, the evil men put baby Zarathustra into burning fire, but the angel Asha-Vahishta which looks after the fire caused the fire to get cold.

Next they placed him in a lane frequented by cattle, with the intention that he would be trampled to death. But a bull rescued him by standing over him and shielded him from stampede. A similar attempt was made by placing him in a passage of horses which also failed. Durasarun continued his efforts to kill Zarathustra. He took him to a wolf cave to be eaten by the beasts. Angels Meher Yazad and Sarosh Yazad came to the baby's rescue in the form of goats who nursed the baby, until he was rescued by his parents. In the end Durasarun tried to perform the murder himself. He entered Zarathustra's house when all were asleep. He was going to strike the baby with his deadly dagger. Right then and there angel Behram Yazad permanently paralyzed and twisted Durasarun's hands as a punishment so that he could never hurt baby Zarathustra again.

Zarathustra grew up to be a good and happy boy. He was kind and always tried to make others happy. Once he saw a starving dog. He fed it bread, gave water and nursed it back to health.

ADAR (SACRET FIRE)

Fire is the symbol of Zarathustrian followers, they are not fire worshippers. The fire symbolizes the fire energy within us.

"The Avestan alphabet was created in the 3rd and 4th centuries AD for writing the hymns of Zarathustra (aka Zoroaster), the Avesta. Many of the letters are derived from the old Pahlavi alphabet of Persia, which itself was derived from the Aramaic alphabet. Avesta language is a sister language of Sanskrit."[18]

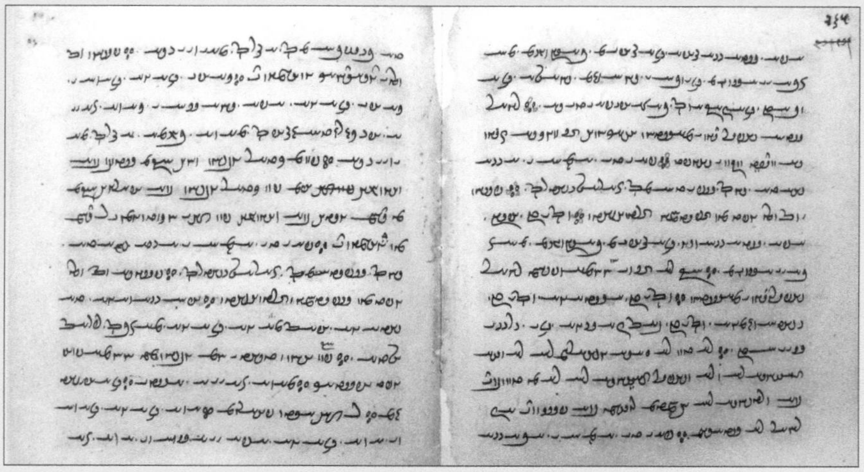

Zarathustra emphasized the battle between good and evil in the world. Each individual is believed to have the free will to choose between these two forces.

Good Thoughts, Good Words and Good Deeds

The basic tenets of the Zarathustrian religion are "Good Thoughts, Good Words and Good Deeds." The pursuit of righteousness (the path of Asha) for the sake of righteousness itself, in every walk of life is the main aim and purpose of life. It is mandatory to regulate one's life by the highest standard of uprightness, truth and purity.

Good Thoughts, Good Words and Good Deeds are basic tenets of Zarathustra's teachings.

Optimistic View

Zarathustra taught that spiritual life and material or worldly life are two aspects of the same basic truth, corresponding to man's higher and lower nature. Life is not a struggle but an opportunity to overcome the base within us, slowly reach out and establish one's higher nature. His viewpoint differs from religious teachings of many other religions in being optimistic rather than taking a pessimistic view as to why human beings have to suffer.

Words Of Wisdom By Zarathustra

"Turn yourself not away from the three best things: Good Thought, Good Word, Good Deed."

"One good deed is worth a thousand prayers."

"With an open mind, seek and listen to all the highest ideals. Consider the most enlightened thoughts. Then choose your path person by person, each for oneself."

The Lamp, The Shadow And The Evil

For his explanation regarding the presence of evil, Zarathustra showed it with the help of a lantern at the court of King Vistaspa, by pointing to the shadow cast by the lamp. According to him, evil does not have a separate identity, but the absence of light is what it is. At all times, one must have unquestioning faith in the divine justice and one has absolute trust in the divine plan which knows what is good for us. There is to be neither doubt nor grievance against God's governance, but humbly submit to his will and honor his orders. This is a very remarkable teaching in the fact that it explains in a new way, the presence of contradictions that we encounter within ourselves and in the universe around us. Till today, they continue to baffle human beings and Zarathustra's teachings so early in the history of man's consciousness, are truly remarkable.

Tehran, Iran. Saraye Roshan building with elaborate sculptural decoration and Zoroastrian Faravahar symbol.

Zoroastrian Symbolism

Faravahar (Divine Glory)

The message of this symbol is that with recognition of one God, with use of wisdom, trustworthiness, wings of Good Thoughts, Good Words and Good Deeds the angelic side of man could free himself from the world of matter and lift towards God.

Head - Represents wisdom.
Raised index finger - Indicates one God.
Ring in left hand - Represents loyalty and faithfulness as well as honoring contracts.
Circle - Reepresents this world of matter.
Two supports - Are the two natures of man (angelic and animal).
Skirt - Represents worldly attachments.
Wings - 3 layers of feathers symbolize Good Thoughts, Good Words, and Good Deeds.

Basic Ideology

Zarathustra's religion is very forward thinking and does not ask its followers to get caught in a guilt trap or torture the body for attaining the truth and higher life. When one does wrong and realizes it, he/she can simply repent from his heart and get on with his/her life. Zarathushtrian religion is not an organized religion. It gives full freedom to an individual to understand and live his/her life in accordance to its principles. Man is not a helpless being tossed around by circumstances beyond control, rather he gets a chance to realize and learn from mistakes. Instead, one grows in understanding and slowly becomes worthy of lending a helping hand in the plan of God.

Zarathustra's Beliefs

When he turned 20 years he felt the need to get closer to God. Leaving home, he spent ten years praying and meditating in the mountains.

At the age of 30, it is said that he had a vision from God. He believed and preached that only one God (Ahura Mazda) was worthy of worship by the people. The other Gods were enemies of the one and true God. He wanted people to understand their relationship with Divine and focused more on moral behavior. The local people and spiritual leaders at that time did not take to Zarathustra's ideas very well, especially, since he classified their Gods as evil. His life was threatened, even his family seemed to have abandoned him, and he was forced to flee his home. Thus, the Prophet, with his twenty-two followers fled the village. They traveled for many weeks until they came across a place where a king named Vishtaspa ruled.

Vishtaspa's Court

King Vishtaspa was no more pleased at hearing of a new faith than the people of Zarathustra's hometown. He had him engaged in a theological

There is only one way to defeat the evil, that is by increasing the Good and only one way to remove the darkness, that is by diffusing the light.

debate with the court priests. Zarathustra defeated all of their arguments, showing how they worshiped false Gods. Hearing such news and offense to Vishtapa's faith, Vishtaspa had Zarathustra imprisoned. Something happened the following day. King Vishtaspa's favorite horse got a mysterious disease. His legs became smaller and weaker each day so that he could no longer stand on his feet. The King summoned the best healers in the land, but no one could cure his horse.

Zarathushtra heard the news and went to the King and said, "I can cure your horse, but first you should grant my four wishes." King Vishtaspa immediately agreed. The four wishes were that first the king, second his queen, third the minister, and all the courtiers to give up the false Gods and join his followers. As Zarathustra's every wish was granted, the legs of the king's horse got healed one by one.

Zarathustra's Teachings

Zoroaster taught that good (Ahura Mazda) and evil (Angra Mainyu) were opposite forces and the battle between them is more or less evenly matched. A person should always be vigilant to align with forces of light.

He taught about free will, opposed the use of the hallucinogenic plant in rituals, polytheism, and over-ritualizing religious ceremonies.

Questions & Answers

What is Zarathustra's teaching based on?
- It is based on idea that good and evil were opposite forces. A person should always choose the forces of good.

What does the fire symbolize for Zarathustrian followers?
- The fire symbolizes the spirit within each one of us.

What did Zarathustra advise to defeat the evil?
- Zarathustra advised that the evil will be destroyed by increasing the good.

With someone close to you, discuss the difference between good and evil and what it means to you.

CONFUCIUS

Confucius was born around 551 BC during the rule of Zhou dynasty, in China. Although there was one ruling family, the real power was in the hands of local warlords. Each warlord ruled a feudal (combination of legal, economic, military and cultural customs) province. Aristocratic scholars, called shi, traveled from one feudal state to another, offering advice on everything from politics to war. The most well-known shi was Confucius. Confucius lived in a time when many states were fighting wars in China. Confucius did not like this and wanted to bring order back into society. His parents were of nobility but became poor when the empire fell apart into feudal provinces. When he was about 15 years old, he became interested in academics. In those days, only the nobles and royals were allowed education. All the teachers were government officials, therefore it was hard for him to find a way to learn. To solve this problem, he went to work for a nobleman. This gave him the opportunity to travel to the imperial capital. Confucius studied and learned until he was the smartest man of his day. People heard of his knowledge and sent their sons to study with him. He was known as the first private teacher in China. Confucius taught anyone who was eager to learn. His ideas, called Confucianism, stressed the need to develop responsibility and moral character through rigid rules of behavior. Confucianism is not a religion; it's a way of behaving, and teaches to make the right choices in life. Confucius' family was part of the growing middle class people of China. They weren't part of the upper class but were considered above the common peasants. This gave him a different outlook on life than the majority of people. He thought that people should be promoted and rewarded based on their talents, rather than in which family they were born into.

Confucius believed that a leader needed to exercise self-discipline in order to remain humble and to treat his followers with compassion.

Early Career

Confucius didn't start out as a wise teacher. He worked in a number of ordinary jobs, including being a shepherd and a clerk, but eventually, Confucius came to work for the government. He started out as the governor of a small town and worked his way up until he became a top-level government advisor.

Philosophy

Confucius did not answer philosophical questions himself. Instead he wanted people to think about problems themselves, learn from past experiences, and consider different viewpoints. Confucius also thought that people should advance in life because they were capable and skilled, not just because they came from influential families. Confucius wanted people to think about other people's welfare more than thinking about accumulating their own wealth. Confucius believed in rules. His many rules dictated the behavior of the people and were meant to prevent them from doing wrong. His students had to learn and obey his many rules. Con-

Shri Mataji Nirmala Devi speaking at the United Nations International Women's Conference in Beijing, China in 1995.

oped his own philosophy and taught it to others. Today, his philosophy is known as Confucianism. His ideas weren't popular until years after his death when they became the guiding philosophy of the Chinese culture for over two thousand years.

Some basic ideas of Confucius

- Treat others kindly.
- Have good manners and follow daily rituals.
- A man should have good morals and ethics.
- Family is important and ancestors are to be respected.
- A true man has the qualities of integrity, righteousness, altruism, and loyalty.
- One should practice moderation in all things.
- He believed in a strong and organized central government.

Later Life

Confucius quit his government job at the age of 51 because he was disappointed that the leaders were not following his teachings. He then traveled throughout China for many years teaching his philosophy. Some of his followers wrote down his ideas in a book that would later be called The Analects of Confucius.

Death

Confucius spent his last few years in his hometown of Qufu teaching his disciples. He died in 479 BC, of natural causes.

Confucianism

Confucius' teachings became the state philosophy of China called Confucianism. The government liked Confucianism because it taught respect for authority and the importance of a strong central government. Confucianism also provided rules for thinking and living. It focused on love for humanity, worship of ancestors, respect for elders, self-discipline, and conformity to rituals.

Confucius' teachings remained an important part of Chinese culture and government up until the 20th century. There are over 2 million known and registered descendants of Confucius today.

Lao Tse Meets Confucius

Lao Tse and Confucius were contemporaries and met each other a few times. According to

Confucious working for government.

Words Of Wisdom By Confucius

"What you do not want done to yourself, do not do to others."

"It does not matter how slowly you go as long as you do not stop."

"Life is really simple, but we insist on making it complicated.

"I hear and I forget. I see and I remember. I do and I understand."

"A gentleman would be ashamed should his deeds not match his words."

"Be the change you want to see in the world."

"Ask yourself constantly, what is the right thing to do?"

"He who cannot define the problem will never find the solution to that problem."

"When it is obvious that the goals cannot be reached, don't adjust the goals, adjust the action steps."

"Shiji," or "The Records of the Grand Historian," one such instance was when Confucius went to Luoyang, the historical capital city, to meet Lao Tse to enquire about rituals and proper etiquette. When Confucious came back from his meeting, he didn't speak for three days. His students grew concerned and asked their teacher what had happened. Confucius said: "I know how a bird can fly. I know how a fish can swim. But I do not know how Lao Tse could rise and fly like a sublime dragon riding on clouds in the sky."

"Birds can fly but will fall at the hunter's arrow. Fish can swim but will be caught by the fisherman. Beasts can run but will drop into people's nets and traps. There is only one thing that is out of man's reach. That is the legendary dragon. A dragon can fly into the sky, ride on clouds, dive into the ocean. A dragon is so powerful, yet so intangible to us. Lao Tse is a dragon, and I will never understand him."

Analects Of Confucius

His students wrote down small stories about him, and things he said. These were put together to make a book called The Analects of Confucius. It has been the basic component of education in Asia for more than two thousand years.

Shri Mataji On Confucius

"Chinese are other very ancient

The Golden Rule

Confucius' social philosophy was based primarily on the principle of "ren" or "loving others" while exercising self-discipline. He believed that ren could be put into action using the Golden Rule.

"What you do not wish for yourself, do not do to others."

- Confucius

people, very wise. Culturally, they are like Indians. They have morality in them. One thing I noticed, they were extremely hospitable, kind and gentle. They are very patriotic people, one has to learn from them.

They had two great philosophers, but the greatest was Lao Tse, who talked about Kundalini, realization, everything. Confucius talked about humanity. So, they believe in Confucius because it suits communism. In Hong Kong there are many Chinese and I asked them what will you do when Hong Kong goes to China, mainland China? They said, "We are Chinese and we'll be with mainland China.

They are very wise. I tell you, Chinese women are very, really very sweet. They don't compete with men. They are very sweet, and they win over men with their sweetness. I also know that they are very sensitive to spirituality. Even their prime minister asked me about spirituality when I went with my husband. And I'm sure one day you'll find your brothers and sisters very closely in China."[19]

Confucious describing Lao Tse.

Establishing Quality People

"Confucius wanted to establish a quality of people, a category of people who would have a feeling for others and we say in samajikata or the public-minded people. Mostly human beings are selfish. They live for their families. At the most they may live for some relations of theirs. But some of them are of a category who rise above that limited sphere and become conscious about the needs of the society. Now when we see somebody dying or getting drowned in in the sea, we find somebody jumping to save that person. In that case who saves is not that person, but the collectivity that is within this gentleman. He feels something of his part and parcel is getting drowned, and he must save that part and parcel, so he jumps to save that. In the same way in the fire, in any catastrophes, when we find people dying to save others, we can explain that innately we are collective beings. Within us there is a collective feeling, and when this collective feeling is expressed in this

Today's look of the city of Luoyang, China, where Lao Tse and Confucius met about 2,500 years ago.

> **"Confucius said that you must become very virtuous, righteous... Humanism he started.**
>
> *-Shri Mataji Nirmala Devi*

manner, you prepare grounds for the divine to work through because the Divine is something that is absolutely collective." [20]

Why Should We Be Good

Confucius is all right, "But for what we should become good?" is the point people will ask. "Why should we be good people?", people can ask such a question. "What is the need to be good, to be balanced?" We too had many like this who talked that, "We have to be in balance, we have to be moral and we have to be righteous people." But for what is this balance we have to find out. This balance is for the ultimate ascent. And unless and until we achieve that ascent, nothing can satisfy us. The fundamental question that we have all over the world, we should say, "Why are we on this earth?"

Then I met many Chinese people also, and I found them to be extremely wise, very balanced, very humble, very sweet and it was such a pleasure to be with them. I felt Chinese are the fit people to get their Self Realization."[21]

Questions & Answers

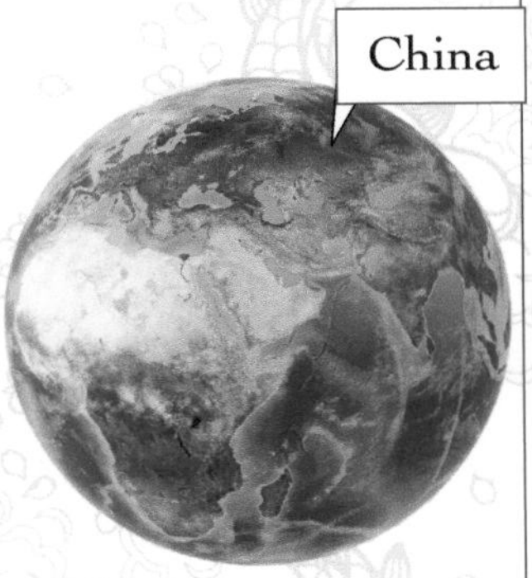

When and where was Confucius born?
- Around 551 BC in China.

Explain the meaning of The Golden Rule by Confucius?
- What you do not wish for yourself, do not do to others.

When Lao Tse met Confucius for the first time, how did he describe Confucius?
- Lao Tse described Confucius as a powerful dragon that he (Lao Tse) would never understand.

What were some basic ideas of Confucius?
- Treat others kindly, have good manners, a man should have good morals and so on,

How did Shri Mataji describe Chinese people? (see page 32)
- They are ancient people, very wise. They are hospitable, kind, and gentle.

Confucius believed that every leader (country, spiritual) should exercise certain qualities. What are those qualities?
- Self-discipline, humility, and compassion.

LAO TSE

Lao Tse was said to have been born as a grown man, with a full grey beard and long ears, which are symbols of wisdom and long life in China. He was born in 4 th century BC. Lao Tse influenced many people throughout the Chinese history. He was a writer, poet, and philosopher (meaning "lover of wisdom"). He had a great deal of influence on Chinese scholars and culture. Lao Tse supported limited government, reasoning that political power could oppose culture and the community. Some historical accounts say he was a peer of the famous Chinese philosopher Confucius. Although Lao Tse does not have as deep of an influence as Confucius does in China, he is still widely respected by the Chinese. Confucius and Lao Tse are the best-known Chinese philosophers in the Western world today.

If you are depressed,
you are living in the past.
If you are anxious,
you are living in the future.
If you are at peace,
you are living in the present.
-Lao Tse

Departure Of Lao Tse

Lao Tse is said to have been tired of life in the Zhou dynasty court as it grew increasingly and morally corrupt. So he left, riding a water buffalo to the western border of the Chinese empire. Although he was dressed as a farmer, the border official recognized him and asked him to write down his wisdom. According to this legend, what Lao Tse wrote be

Tao Te Ching
(The Book Of The Way)

Tao Te Ching delivers 81 verses on how to live in the world with goodness and integrity: an important kind of wisdom in a world where many people believe such a thing to be impossible.

He who stands on tiptoedoesn't stand firm.
He who rushes ahead doesn't go far.
He who tries to shine dims his own light.
He who defines himself can't know
who he really is.

He who has power over others
can't empower himself.
He who clings to his work will create nothing
that endures.
If you want to accord with the Tao, just do your job,
then let go.

If you want to become full, let yourself be empty.
If you want to be reborn, let yourself die.
If you want to be given everything,
give everything up.

The Master has no possessions.
The more he does for others, the happier he is.
The more he gives to others, the wealthier he is.
- *Tao Te Ching*

Lao Tse was said to have been born as a grown man with a full grey beard and long ears, symbols of wisdom and long life.

Lao Tse in China has very beautifully described TAO, meaning the Kundalini. This Tao is something like the Kundalini of Sahaja Yoga.

came the sacred text called the Tao Te Ching. After writing this, Lao Tse is said to have crossed the border and disappeared from history, perhaps to become a hermit.

Shri Mataji On Lao Tse

"This country (China) has been endowed with great philosophers, I would say the greatest was Lao Tse, because humanism was for the preparation of human beings for their ascent about which Lao Tse had spoken. But because of the subtle subject it was not described in such a clear-cut manner as I am talking to you. It is such a pleasure for me to talk to this gathering here. After traveling all over the world, I realize that China is one of the best countries as far as spirituality is concerned."[22]

Tao Description

"Tao means what you are, and he (Lao Tse) describes very nicely that when you are that what, happens. Now, the gap was how to achieve that state, how to reach that state was not given. He (Lao Tse) only described people who were Tao, who were realized souls, who were of what level I wonder. I was surprised that he never said about kundalini, but he talked about the river, Yangtse. That it is Yangtse river, you see in a symbolic way, he was more poetic. But ultimately reaching the ocean, that river becomes the ocean and then what are the qualities of the ocean he described so beautifully. Now, I would say you all have become supposing the ocean. So, are you behaving like the ocean? Are you understanding your capacity to be an ocean? What is an ocean is: look at the ocean, it has its own boundaries, maryadas, it doesn't cross. If you try to push it one side, it will come outside. So you are, you have to be in your marayadas. That's very important that you should be in your balance."[23]

"In Sahaja Yoga, Tao refers to the balancing of right and left side. When this balance is maintained the healing energy is able to travel on the central channel to integrate and nourish all the energy centers and ultimately keep us in harmony with the balance of nature. The left side caters for our emotions, for our past, our desires. The right side caters for our action physical and mental. If we indulge into one too much and go

Yin & Yang

Yin and yang represent the masculine and feminine or right and left side of our psyche. The yang being masculine active right side and yin being the feminine passive side. Viewed in the light of Sahaja Yoga, we can see how this is parallel to the subtle system. In Sahaja Yoga Tao refers to the balancing of right and left side. When this balance is maintained the healing energy is able to travel on the central channel to integrate and nourish all the energy centers and ultimately keep us in harmony with the balance of nature.

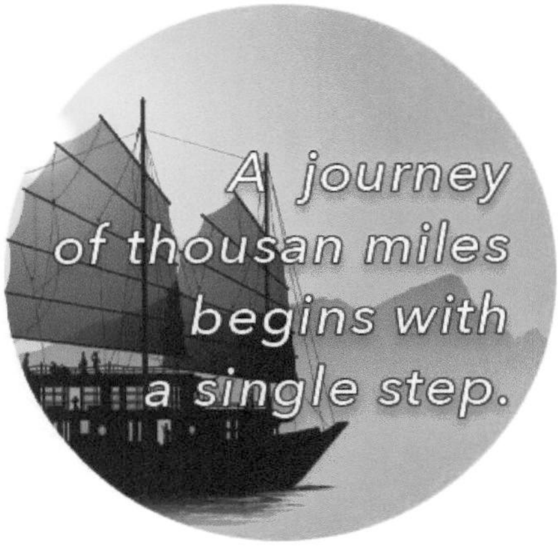
A journey
of thousan miles
begins with
a single step.

too far with it you develop an imbalance within yourself."[24]

Yangtze River And Tao

"Now, you see, for this, the best thing is to know about Tao which is your specialty it's Chinese in which he describes, you see, Tao; Lao Tse describes the journey through the river Yangtze. I've been Myself to see that. So he says on the side or the banks there are beautiful, very beautiful mountains and beautiful trees and it's so beautiful that you feel like jumping out of the boat and going to these gardens and these mountains. But what your aim is to go through this, Tao, means the Yangtze river, towards the river. In the beginning, maybe there are some currents flowing, maybe you might lose faith in yourself. But by the time you reach near the sea, it becomes very silent and you have to go to the sea, that's the point is. So, you see, all these are there; these are just enticing... It's all right you see but it's nothing important because all these will keep you on a mental level. You'll be always thinking, "What is this vision? What is that?" There's nothing to be on the mental level, you have to beyond, all right? If you don't see, you don't bother about it, they'll disappear."[25]

Laws Of God

"Confucius said that you must become very virtuous, righteous. Humanism he started. But now they found out that now they are going too much towards it. So Lao Tse came. You see they had to work it out, because some people move like a pendulum on one side and then they had to move them on other side. Lao Tse came, he talked about Tao. So, all these great prophets tried to give you a balance, to give you the proper sense of law of God."[26]

Nature Is Like Artist's Painting

"In your country you had very great philosophers once upon a time. Of course, you believe in humanism; but there was another great philosopher who was called Lao Tse. He was of a very high spirituality; like a great incarnation of a Master. What He has written about, described about the Yangtze River is very interesting, because I went through the Yangtze River Myself. And He calls it Tao. He is actually talking about Kundalini. He was a poet, so whatever He has described is rather subtle. And maybe they must have thought that it is better to understand other people, rather than the Tao written by Lao-Tse. But all over the world you will find it is Tao which people respect very much, and they always like to interpret the meaning of the word "Tao."

Really, symbolically He has described that this river Yangtze is a difficult river to go through. And the surroundings, the banks of this river, are extremely beautiful. For twelve hours I was sitting outside watching

---

"Water is fluid, soft, and yielding. But water will wear away rock, which is rigid and cannot yield. As a rule, whatever is fluid, soft, and yielding will overcome whatever is ridged and hard. This is another paradox: what is soft is strong."

- Lao Tse

Calligraphed name of Lao Tse in Chinese Hanzi.

"The Yangtze River is the longest river in Asia, the third-longest in the world and the longest in the world to flow entirely within one country. It flows 6,300 km in a generally easterly direction to the East China Sea. For thousands of years, the river has been used for water, irrigation, sanitation, transportation, industry, boundary-marking and war."[28]

the beauty of the banks. I've never seen such beautiful mountains and trees. The thing is this: that in the beginning it's a very difficult river, whole movement of nature is like an artist's painting. And many of your paintings are impressed by the kind of banks that I saw. But the symbolist here are lots of currents, they form lots of circles, very heavy type, and is very difficult to climb. For quite some time you have to pass very carefully. Just in the few hours when it reaches the sea, it becomes calm, absolutely calm. In the same way, the Tao that He describes is, in the beginning, according to Him, rather difficult. But when it reaches near the sea, it calms down. It is a remarkable thing how He could see the Kundalini so well defined - as this Yangtze River. It shows what a poet He must have been, and how highly developed, spiritually."[27]

"Mastering others is strength. Mastering yourself is true power."

- Lao Tse

Words Of Wisdom By Lao Tse

"Do the difficult things while they are easy and do the great things while they are small."

"Kindness in words creates confidence. Kindness in thinking creates profoundness. Kindness in giving creates love."

"To the mind that is still, the whole universe surrenders."

"If you are depressed, you are living in the past.
If you are anxious, you are living in the future.
If you are at peace, you are living in the present."

"Time is a created thing. To say, 'I don't have time' is like saying, 'I don't want to do something."

"Nature does not hurry, yet everything is accomplished."

"If there is to be peace in the world, there must be peace in the heart."

"Care about what other people think and you will always be their prisoner."

Questions & Answers

When and where was Lao Tse born?
- In the 4th century BC in China.

Lao Tse described Tao in a beautiful way. What is Tao?
- Tao is Kundalini. Lao Tse described the Kundalini.

What does the symbol Yin and Yang represent?
- Yin and Yang represents feminine and masculine energy, the left and the right side.

What was Lao Tse's advice to Confucius?
- Lao Tse advised Confucius to give up forcing information and instead let go of everything and follow the natural Tao.

What was Lao Tse's profession?
- He was a writer, poet, and philosopher, as well as Keeper of the Archives.

What was the main message of Lao Tse?
- His message was simplicity, recognition, non-action. He was a person who sought to answer questions about humans and their place in the universe.

SOCRATES

Socrates was an ancient Greek philosopher. He is respected as a brilliant thinker and teacher with a great thirst for knowledge. Socrates is remembered for developing ideas and thoughts that led to the Western culture that exists today. Socrates was born 469 BC in Athens, Greece. He trained as a stonemason, like his father, but later he decided to spend his time searching for knowledge. He did this by spending his time discussing ideas with his friends. They would meet in public places, and people passing by would join in the discussion.

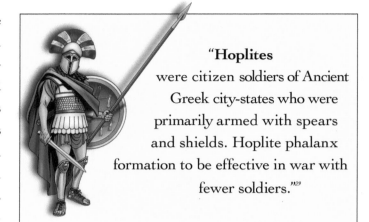

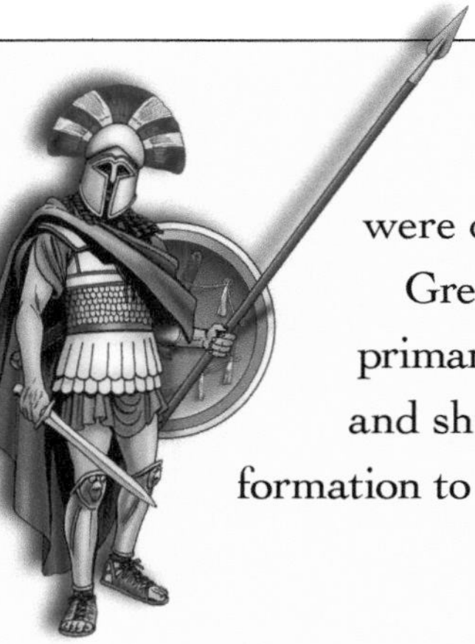

"**Hoplites** were citizen soldiers of Ancient Greek city-states who were primarily armed with spears and shields. Hoplite phalanx formation to be effective in war with fewer soldiers."[29]

As required by the Athenian law, Socrates also served as hoplite or citizen soldier at the Peloponnesian War (431–404 BC), fighting with shield, long spear and face mask.

During the war, he showed tremendous courage, a trait that remained with him for the rest of his life. He increasingly developed an interest in philosophy.

Philosophy

He asked his students questions about a topic, helping them to discover where their knowledge or beliefs were flawed. He used this method—now called the Socratic Method—to reveal wisdom. For example, he argued that he had no fear of death. He reasoned that he had no knowledge of what came afterwards and could not fear what he did not know.

Gradually, he started becoming popular, especially among the city's youth, most famous of them being the philosopher Plato. With long hair, upturned nose and bulging eyes, he moved around the city, barefooted and unwashed, asking questions to the elite and to the commoners alike, seeking to arrive at the truth. His young disciples enjoyed the debates, relishing the fact that he always defeated those who were considered wise. In spite of his fame and popularity, Socrates did not consider himself wise.

Socrates was a man of principle, who often stood against the political system that operated in ancient Greece at the time. He also angered many people by his method of questioning since it often showed that people were not as wise as they claimed to be.

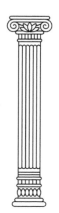

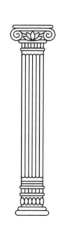

Socrates believed that people should strive for goodness rather than material interests such as wealth. He encouraged others to focus more on companionship and making connections with other people because he felt this was the ideal path for individuals to come together as a group.

Know thys
Σ

The Death Of Socrates

Despite being advised not to, Socrates decided to stand up against the current norms of society and politics in Athens. He believed, as a loyal citizen of Athens, it was his duty to pinpoint the shortcomings in their way of life, even if it questioned the beliefs that had been followed for centuries. In 399 BC, he was brought to trial, being charged with corrupting the minds of young people and not giving religion enough respect. Despite his noble intentions, Socrates had rubbed off some members of the nobility on the wrong side, thus eventually leading to his execution.

The jury believed that he was a dangerous man, and he was sentenced to death by poisoning. In the event, friends, followers, and students encouraged Socrates to flee Athens, action which the Athenians expected of him. Being a man of principles, Socrates refused to flout the law and escape his legal responsibility to Athens. Socrates never rejected his teachings and as a result he died after drinking a cup of deadly hemlock.

At the time of Socrates people had evolved, they were a much better people so he could talk to them about something of wisdom, of honesty, of righteousness, of peace. Of so many things he talked and he could talk because people were worthy of that.

Diwali Puja 1999, Delphi, Greece

Shri Mataji On Socrates

"Socrates has told us that we have to leave our body for the second life and that when we live on this earth, when we live as human beings on this earth, we have to keep ourselves in such a way that we do not spoil our being. That we have a sustenance within us, a quality which makes us human beings, by which we can be called as human beings.

What is the difference between human beings and animals? As so many others also have said the same thing, that we are human beings, because we are human beings, we have to maintain a certain amount of sustenance. Socrates had said one more thing, that there are Deities within us and we have to look after those deities, we have to keep them pleased. Sustenance means the one we sustain within us." But there were two types of seeking going on alongside – two types of seeking. One was the devotion on the left-hand side, and on the right-hand side was the, we can say the intellectual. And devotion came to people because they felt there is something beyond this human life which thought of the creator – being there."[30]

His Wisdom Was Well Known

"Socrates, who came here in such a condition when people were really, absolutely ignorant, in the complete darkness of ignorance. They could not understand him. They could not understand Socrates at all and so, like any other Primordial Master, he was ill-treated by the people who were surrounding him. But of course, he was a Primordial Master and his wisdom is well-known and he created out of him disciples, but none of them could go anywhere near his wisdom. They started their own theories, own styles, and that is how we find the accent from philosophy that was Socrates' aim, gradually came into the political and then into the economic side. So, the attention was moved from philosophy to economics today, not towards the philosophy, which was

Socrates believed that human choice was driven by a wish to be happy and the ultimate happiness comes from knowing oneself.

What Is The Socratic Method

"It is teaching through step-by-step questions that are designed to lead the student to the truth. The principle underlying the Socratic method is that students learn through the use of critical thinking, and logic. This technique involves finding holes in their own theories and then patching them up.This often-rapid-fire exchange takes place in front of the entire class so students can practice thinking and making arguments on their feet. It also helps them master the art of speaking in front of large groups."[31]

Words Of Wisdom By Socrates

"The only true wisdom is to know that you know nothing."

"Strong minds discuss ideas, average minds discuss events, weak minds discuss people."

"To find yourself, think for yourself."

"A good man treats women with honor."

"What has reached you was never meant to miss you, and what has missed you was never meant to reach you."

"Make things easy for people and not difficult. Give people good news and bring them joy, and do not turn them away."

"The best among you is the one who doesn't harm others with his tongue and hands."

"Nature has given us two ears, two eyes, and but one tongue-to the end that we should hear and see more than we speak."

> **Contentment is natural wealth, luxury is artificial powerty.**
> - Socrates

established by Socrates. We can say Socrates was the one Primordial Master, after Abraham and Moses, who really made it a very clear-cut understanding about spirituality."[32]

World Peace

"World Peace can be achieved only when people in charge of world affairs get their self-realization. They are leaders of different countries

and through a Sahaja relation they will respect and love each other. They will be like benevolent kings described by Socrates, who will think of global peace. Today it seems as if the whole world is ablaze with war."[33]

Interesting Facts

- Socrates stuck out - he chose not to pursue money, power or fame, but to live in poverty as a street philosopher.
- The Socratic Method was genius at work - Instead of lecturing students on the nature of knowledge, He'd socialized all day in the marketplace of Athens and asked people questions. Socrates did not argue that he had the answer to any question being posed — from the nature of knowledge to the meaning of life. To him, the Socratic Method was an exercise in breaking down false assumptions and exposing ignorance so that the individual being questioned — not Socrates — could arrive at their own conclusion.
- Socrates asked questions - he asked questions and allowed people to think for themselves. Example of his questions: "What is the point in battle ships and city walls, unless the people building them and protected by them are happy?" Or: "The unexamined life is not worth living.

Greece's True Responsibility & Place In The World

"Now, you have to understand that you people have a very big responsibility because you're strategically placed in Greece, you see. Greece and Turkey, both are very important. First of all, you are the bridge between the eastern side and the western side and everybody is interested in, somehow or other, managing and controlling these two areas so that they could control eastern and western side. I mean the western countries specially. Now the greatest danger that you have now is that this western cul-

City of Athens

ture may try to grab you and which is very dangerous. To understand it, you have to know that you are people coming from a very great tradition, ancient people of ages just like Indians, and there is so much you can do to improve the culture of Europe by your own behavior. Tourists are coming and they see the behavior of the Greeks. The Europeans think that Greeks can be very easily influenced by their culture, by their cheap life."[34]

Country Full Of Vibrations

"It's a very great day for me to see so many Sahaja Yogis here who are from this country, Greece. When first I came to Greece, I told my husband that this country is full of vibrations and there have been many evolved souls in this country, but perhaps the people have lost their atmosphere and one day Sahaja Yoga heritage, but the vibrations are in the should prosper here very much."[35]

Athena

"So, the circumstances made the reactions of the people, also the awareness of human beings. So many things worked it out. Say, for example, when Athena came on this earth, her job was to create an integrated force which will have the whole Chaitanya spread like an integrated force. So that when it will be all disintegrated later on, it can integrate. So, the Greeks have a job, special job, is to intergrate. You have to integrate people which are left-sided and right-sided."[36]

> **"The secret of change is to focus all of your energy, not on fighting the old, but on building the new."**
> - Socrates

Questions & Answers

What is the Socratic Method?
- Socrates asked his students questions about a topic, helping them to discover where their knowledge or beliefs were flawed.

What did Shri Mataji say about Greece when She visited this country?
- Shri Mataji said that Greece is full of vibrations and there have been many evolved souls in this country.

Shri Mataji has said that there is only one way to achieve world peace. Explain.
- According to Shri Mataji, World Peace can be achieved only when people in charge of world affairs get their self-realization.

> "THE ONLY TRUE WISDOM IS IN KNOWING YOU KNOW NOTHING."
> Socrates

Why did Socrates ask questions from his disciples?
- Socrates asked questions and allowed people to think for themselves.

- Socrates believed that human choice was driven by a certain wish. What wish was it?
- Human choice was driven by a wish to be happy.

Prophet Muhammad

Prophet Muhammad was not yet born when his father died. He was born into a poor but respectable family of the Quraysh tribe. His family was active in Meccan politics and trade. After his father's death, Amina, his mother, was left alone. When the little boy was born, she was very happy. She thought her baby was very special. There was a custom among the Arabs of that time of bringing up little children in the desert. It was considered best for them. They were sent to the desert, accompanied by women, who looked after them as their own.

In his early teens, Muhammad worked in a camel caravan, following in the footsteps of many people his age, born of meager wealth. Working for his uncle, he gained experience in commercial trade.

He traveled all over, from the Mediterranean Sea to the Indian Ocean. Over time, Muhammad earned a reputation of being honest and sincere, acquiring the nickname "al-Amin" meaning faithful or trustworthy.

One day, Muhammad went to Syria with his uncle in a trading caravan. During this trip he met a monk, who predicted that Muhammad would one day become a prophet.

At age 40, Muhammad began to have revelations from Allah that later became the basis of the Koran and the foundation of Islam. By 630 AD Muhammad had unified most of Arabia under a single religion.

Many of the tribes living in the Arabian Peninsula at the time were nomadic. A 'nomad' is someone who travels from place to place, without staying in one place for a long time. Nomadic hunter-gatherer tribes follow the animals, they hunt, live in tents of yurts, and trade goods while crossing large, often desert like areas. Most tribes of that time were polytheistic. Polytheism is the worship of, or belief in multiple deities. Islamic tradition claims that the first people to believe in Muhammad were his wife, Khadija and his close friend Abu Bakr. Muhammad soon had a small following, initially encountering no opposition. Most people in Mecca either ignored him or mocked

---

"At the time of resurrection, your hands will speak."

-Prophet Muhammad

"What actions are most excellent?
To gladden the heart of human beings,
to feed the hungry, to help the afflicted,
to lighten the sorrow of the sorrowful,
and to remove the sufferings of the injured."

-Bukhari

him as yet another prophet. However, when his message condemned idol worship and polytheism, many of Mecca's tribal leaders began to regard Muhammad and his message as a threat. In addition to going against long standing beliefs, the condemnation of idol worship had economic consequences for merchants who catered to the thousands of pilgrims who came to Mecca every year. This was especially true for members of Muhammad's own tribe, the Quraysh, who were also the guardians of the Kaaba. Sensing a threat, Mecca's merchants and leaders offered Muhammad money to abandon his preaching, but he refused.

Increasingly, the resistance to Muhammed and his followers grew. In 622 AD, they were eventually forced to emigrate from Mecca to Medina, a city 260 miles to the north. This event marks the beginning of the Muslim calendar. The Prophet Muhammad was instrumental in bringing an end to a civil war raging among several of the city's tribes. Muhammad settled in Medina, building his Muslim community. He gradually found acceptance amongst people and gained more followers.

> **"Muhammad Sahib has also said that you have to become the pir. Pir means realized soul."**
>
> *-Shri Mataji Nirmala Devi*

Between 624 and 628 AD, the Muslims were involved in a series of battles for their survival. In the final major confrontation, the Battle of the Trench and Siege of Medina, Muhammad and his followers prevailed, and a treaty was signed. By now, the Prophet Muhammad had plenty of forces, and the balance of power had shifted away from the Meccan leaders to him. In 630 AD, the Muslim army marched into Mecca, taking the city with minimum casualties. Most of the Meccan population converted to Islam. Shortly after the conflict with Mecca was finally settled, Prophet Muhammad fell ill for several days and died at age of 62 years.

Muhammad was very religious. One day he visited a sacred site near Mecca. On this pilgrimage in 610 AD, he was meditating in a cave on Mount Jabal Al-Nour. The Angel Gabriel appeared to him and relayed these word of God: "Recite in the name of your Lord who creates, creates man from a clot! Recite, for your lord is most generous...."

The Battle of the Trench

In the year 627 AD the Mekkans made another great effort to destroy the Muslims with the help of the Jews and the desert tribes of Ghatafan. This great army of 10,000 men, 4,000 camels and 300 horses marched towards Madina. News of the preparations reached Muhammad, who advised to dig deep, wide trenches around the city. These trenches gave the Muslims the advantage of defeating enemy armies and of suffering fewer casualties. The trenches also surprised the enemy army. They had no choice but to wait for 27 days and then lay siege to the city. Suddenly, when the Muslims really needed help, the weather changed. Strong winds, thunder and heavy rain storms made the enemy flee in disarray.

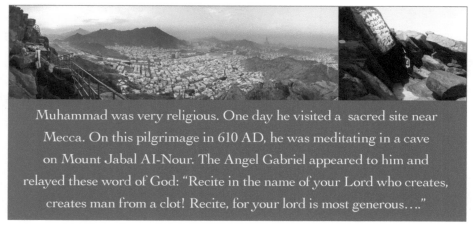

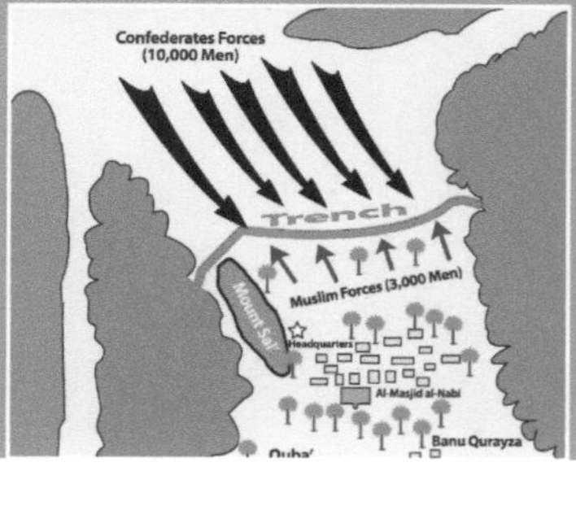

Sharia Law
"Moreover Mohammad Sahib taught of Sharia which was acturally given by Moses to the Jews, but the Jews gave it up."

Sharia (meaning "the right path") regulates public behavior, private behavior, and even private beliefs. Compared to other legal codes, the Sharia law also prioritizes punishment over rehabilitation and favors corporal (physical) and capital punishments (death penalty) over imprisonment.

gave amnesty to many of the Meccan leaders who had opposed him and pardoned many others. Most of the Meccan population converted to Islam. Prophet Muhammad and his followers then proceeded to destroy all of the statues of pagan gods in and around the Kaaba. Shortly after the conflict with Mecca was finally settled, Prophet Muhammad fell ill for several days and died at age of 62 years.

Shri Mataji On Muhammad

"Fatima (an incarnation of Shri Vishnumaya), she was a daughter of Muhammad. She had two sons and was eventually killed by fanatics. Fatima was the embodiment of Shri Gruha Lakshmi. She resides in our left Nabhi. For all the diseases that are connected with the spleen, all the problems that are connected with your left Nabhi, can be only corrected by Fatima. So you have to keep Fatima awakened within yourself. In the Islamic culture a housewife was given a very, very important place.

At the time of Muhammad Sahib, there were struggles and fights and wars going on between different tribes. As a result, many, many men were killed. Only the old people survived and also so many women. This is the reason why Muhammad said that you can marry four wives, five wives. He understood that unless and until women are kept absolutely chaste, absolutely pure, there cannot be the Kingdom of God. This is how a woman, housewife is shown to be so powerful that though she is in the house, looks to be just a mother, but how powerful she is.

Fatima did not go out of her house, she remained a housewife. She made her children grow up in the way that they had to fight the war against fanaticism."[37]

Your Hands Will Speak

"Samayaachar." "Samaya" means "time" and "aachar" means "behaving". And Muhammad clearly said about the resurrection time many years. He has talked about resurrection much more than he talked about doomsday and he said: "At the time of resurrection, your hands will speak clearly. And next the feet will start to speak." [38]

GOOD CHARACTER MELTS AWAY SIN JUST AS THE SUN MELTS AWAY ICE

- Prophet Muhammad

Allah Ho Akbar

"Muhammad Sahib has said 'Allah ho Akbar' he means nothing but he was talking about Shri Krishna. There is no fight between Muhammad Sahib and Shri Krishna. You will be amazed because Muhammad Sahib was nobody else but the incarnation of

Words Of Wisdom By Prophet Muhammad

"You do not do evil to those who do evil to you, but you deal with them with forgiveness and kindness."

"Riches are not from an abundance of worldly goods but from a contented mind."

"The best of houses is the house where an orphan gets love and kindness."

"Seek knowledge from cradle to the grave."

"A good man treats women with honor."

"What has reached you was never meant to miss you, and what has missed you was never meant to reach you."

"Make things easy for people and not difficult. Give people good news and bring them joy, and do not turn them away."

"The best among you is the one who doesn't harm others with his tongue and hands."

Dattatreya himself. There is no difference between them. If you see the history in Sahaj yoga, people are surprised when I say that all these incarnations reincarnated themselves. They are one principle."[39]

Mecca Stone

"It is said that whatever is created by Mother Earth or by the sky should not be reproduced by human beings and be worshipped. For example, even in Mecca, we have got Makeshwarashiva (Shiva, the God of Mecca); in our puranas, He's described as Makeshwarashiva itself. That's why in Mecca we have a stone which was respected by Muhammad Sahib, you see, this subtle point should be seen; that it was a swayambhu one and it is a Makeshwarashiva itself was there. So He was respected. And every stone is not created by the Mother Earth; because the Mother Earth, whatever she creates has got a coefficient which Muhammad Sahib, being an incarnation of Adi Guru or the Primordial Master could see and said that, "This is the stone, is to be kept here and go round that stone."[40]

Be Moral People

"Now, we have to understand that whatever Muhammad Sahib has done is for our good, for our

Kaaba

The Black Stone is a rock set into the eastern corner of the Kaaba, the ancient building in the center of the Grand Mosque in Mecca, Saudi Arabia. The Black Stone was originally a single piece of rock but today consists of several pieces that have been cemented together. They are surrounded by a silver frame which is fastened by silver nails to the Kaaba's outer wall. The entire building is covered by black cloth and is regularly replaced when it wears out.

benevolence. All this he told us to be moral people, because we have to be moral. If we are immoral then our humanity goes away. But he said, you have to have Rahmân (feminine aspect of God: mercy), Rahîm (masculine aspect of God: compassion for the good) all the time he talked about love."[41]

Cancer And Bhavsagar

"When someone gets cancer, he can be cured by either Nanak Sahib or Mohammad Sahib, no one else. Because what we call void, is known to doctors. We call it Bhavsagar. Dattatreya, who is Adi Guru, who helps us in crossing Bhavsagar, where all gurus are present. Unless you take the name of one of them, you are not going to be free from problems of Bhavsagar, which manifest as cancer."[42]

Don't Drink Alcohol

"Muhammad Sahib came with all His powers... That's why some people don't understand why Christ didn't talk against alcoholism, because He came at this point, at the ego point, Mohammad Sahib came awareness, which is sustained by your liver and the liver gets spoilt and that's why they were against it... For example, see a train is moving, all right? Then it stops at a point. And whatever is the problem at that point, is done by the person in charge. If the train doesn't move from there, how will it reach the station? Now will you say that the reaching the station is the last stop? Every stop is important for the station, for the train to move. So everybody has played a very important role, equally important, there is nothing like one person being important, that... we don't think like that."[43]

Did You Know

Prophet Muhammad prohibited animal abuse. He said that the one who kills an animal for sport is cursed. He also corrected people who overloaded their horses or camels and told them to "Fear Allah concerning these animals that cannot speak". He also taught that, people can go to heaven when they cared for animals.

Questions & Answers

When and where was Prophet Muhammad born?
- 570 AD in Mecca, today Saudi Arabia.

Who was Fatima and how is she related to Prophet Muhammad?
- She was the incarnation of Shri Vishnumaya. She was the daughter of Prophet Muhammad.

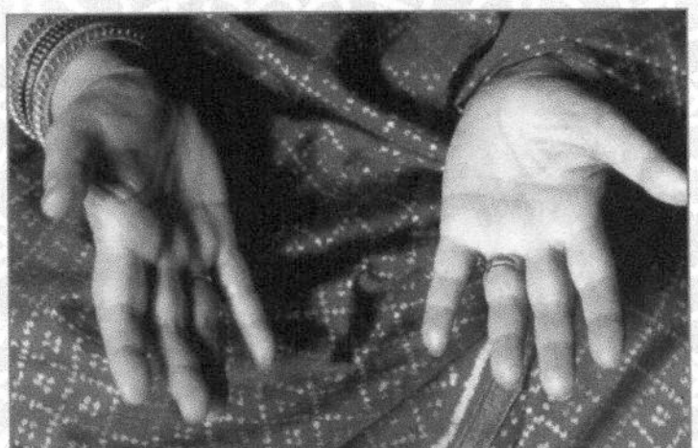

The city of Mecca has a stone on display called Kaaba. What is this stone?
- It is a svayambhu, a creation of Mother Earth, that emits vibrations.

The Prophet Muhammad said that at the time of resurrection, your hands will speak. What does it mean?
- That one should get self-realization and feel vibrations in hands and feet.

What was the message of Prophet Muhammad?
- His message was of the oneness with God and the ultimate submission to God.

GURU NANAK

Guru Nanak was born in Rāi Bhoi Kī Talvandī, present day Pakistan in 1469. As a young boy Nanak had big dreams of what the world might be like without all the fighting he saw around him. People in his village and the surrounding villages were always arguing about which God was real and whose ideas were right. Nanak was fed up with it all, and he wondered if there was a better way to live. He started spending time with the holy men who lived in the forest just outside his village, talking with them about God. Thinking deeply about what they said, he started writing poetry. Nanak's father, however, thought this was a silly idea and wanted his son to be rich and successful.

As time went on Nanak grew up, got married, and had a family of his own. He had two sons whom he loved dearly. But he still hadn't forgotten the dreams of a peaceful world that he had as a boy. Everyday Nanak went down to the river to meditate early in the morning. It was his favorite part of the day. But one day something happened to him that would change his life forever. Nanak had gone down to the river to meditate and take bath as usual. As was his custom, he undressed, left his clothes in a neat pile and plunged into the deep refreshing waters. A few moments later, Nanak didn't reappear to scrub himself clean as he usually did. Several more minutes went by and, there was no

Even Kings and emperors with heaps of wealth and vast dominion cannot compare with an ant filled with the love of God.

When Nanak was a boy, he was sent to the market to buy goods and to resell them for a profit. On the way to the market, Nanak saw many people who were poor and realized they needed the money more than he did, so he gave it away. Nanak used to say that even when he was asleep he was with God.

On one occasion, Nanak was sleeping under a tree in the forest near his home. As the sun rose in the sky, Nanak was in danger of being burned by the rays of the sun due to sleeping outside and not in a sheltered or shaded spot. A cobra suddenly slid out of the forest and drew itself up tall with its black hood wide open, but instead of striking Nanak, it used its hood to provide shade. People in the village began to realize that Nanak was very special.

sign of him. The other bathers in the river began to panic and alerted his family. They searched everywhere along the river bank, in the woods, anywhere they could think of where he might have gone. After two days had gone by, his family feared that he might

A cobra protecting Guru Nanak.

Disappearance of Guru Nanak.

have drowned. Everyone in the village was sad. They all loved Nanak because he was kind, honest, and good. Early on the third morning, after his disappearance, something amazing happened. Right next to the place where Nanak swam, they found his clothes in a neat pile. The river water was rippling and then to everyone's surprise Nanak emerged from the same spot where he had plunged deep under the water.

> "Guru Nanak came down to tell about Mohammed Sahib and about other gurus and to bring unity of Hindus and Muslims."
>
> *- Shri Mataji Nirmala Devi*

Nanak wasn't the same. His eyes were shining more brightly and his face was filled with serene joy. People were overjoyed to see him alive, healthier and happier than they had ever seen him before.

They were puzzled because Nanak didn't seem to want to tell them anything about what had happened during the three days he was missing. However, Nanak's actions during that time spoke louder than any words. He gave up his well-paid job and shared all his belongings amongst the poorest people of the village. When Nanak finally spoke, he explained that while he was in the river he had seen a vision of God and that God had given him a message for everyone. Nanak wanted to share it with as many people as possible. He made four long journeys and took the message that God had given him everywhere he went. As time went by people started to call him "Guru" which means teacher. Guru Nanak travelled across South Asia and Middle East to spread his teachings. He proclaimed the existence of one God, and taught his followers that every human being can reach out to God through meditation and other pious (honorable) practices. Interestingly, Guru Nanak did not support monasticism (a religious way of life in which one renounces worldly pursuits to devote oneself fully to spiritual work) and asked his followers to lead a life of honest householder. His teachings were immortalized in the form of 974 hymns, which came to be known as 'Guru Granth Sahib.'

As a child, Nanak would astonish many with his intelligence and his interest in divine subjects. For his 'upanayana' ritual (is one of the traditional ceremonies marking the acceptance of a student by a guru), he was asked to wear the sacred thread made of three strands, but Nanak simply refused to wear the thread. When the priest insisted, young Nanak

Guru Nanak's Message

- God has made everything and He sees everyone as equals.
- God loves everyone, it doesn't matter to Him what they look like or how much money they have.
- God loves all, whether it is a girl or a boy or whether they are old or young.
- God wants people to live their life peacefully with each other as He intended.

Words Of Wisdom By Guru Nanak

"Before becoming a Muslim, a Hindu, a Sikh, or a Christian, let's become a human first.

"All living beings have come from God. Let us live together in peace and harmony."

"God is one, but He has innumerable forms. He is the creator of all and He himself takes the human form."

"Hundreds of thousands of clever tricks, but not even one of them will go along with you in the end."

"Those who have loved are those that have found God."

"By conquering your mind, you conquer the world."

"Speak only that which will bring you honor."

took everyone by surprise by asking for a thread that is sacred in every sense of the word. He wanted the thread to be made of mercy, contentmen and wanted continence and truth to hold the three sacred threads together. Guru Nanak taught that every human being is capable of attaining spiritual perfection which will ultimately lead them to God. He also said that rituals and priests are not required in order to have direct access to God. In his teachings, Guru Nanak emphasized that God has created many worlds and also created life itself. Nanak also urged them to lead a spiritual life by serving others and to lead an honest life without indulging in exploitation or fraud. Guru Nanak's preaching came at a time when there were conflicts between various religions. Mankind was so intoxicated with pride and ego that people had started fighting against each other in the name of God and religion. Hence, Guru Nanak began his teachings by saying that there are no Hindus and no Muslims. He condemned slavery, racial discrimination and said that all are equal. Guru Nanak is one of the most important religious figures to have contributed to women's empowerment in India. Guru Nanak appealed to his followers to respect women and to treat them as their equal. He said a man is always bound to women and that without women there would be no creation on earth.

KHANDA

Khanda is a symbol of Sikhism. It is made up of the khanda, a double-edged sword; the chakkar (ring), which reminds Sikhs to remain within the rule of God; and two crossed kirpans, swords that represent spiritual authority and political power.

The Story Of Guru Nanak And Wali Kandhari

While on his way back home, Guru Nanak attracted people of the surrounding areas by his teachings. He told people that there was only one God but we call him by different names. Guru Nanak also explained that religions are different paths which ultimately lead us to the same destination - God Almighty.

People of both Hindu and Muslim community started coming to him to seek his blessings. The number of people who would come to see Guru Nanak were increasing every day. A priest named Wali Kandhari lived on the top of a hill near where Guru Nanak settled for a while. Wali was a very greedy and arrogant person.

A spring of fresh water flowed from where he lived. The spring was the only source of water for the poor villagers. The priest used to take money from anyone who wanted to use the water. Wali Kandhari noticed the growing popularity of Guru Nanak and grew jealous of him. He wanted people to come to him for advice and knowledge instead of going to Guru Nanak. In order to drive Guru Nanak out of the village, Kandhari stopped the flow of water and cut its supply to the people. A group of locals went to Wali Kandhari and requested him to let the villagers use the water again, but Kandhari was blinded by hatred and he angrily fended of the villagers. He taunted them and told them to ask their Guru Nanak for water instead.

The villagers approached Guru Nanak and narrated the incident to him. He convinced them not to lose hope in God, because God will take care of them. After explaining to the villagers not to lose hope, Guru Nanak sent his disciple Mardana to Wali. Mardana went to Kandhari and politely asked him to let the water flow to the town. But Kandhari was as angry as ever. He insulted Mardana instead and said if he has no money then he cannot use water. He said to him to ask water from his beloved Guru Nanak instead.

When Mardana came back disappointed and told Guru Nanak about what had happened, Guru Nanak asked Mardana to go back to Khandari again and ask for water yet again, and to tell Kandhari that God has made water and air free for all.

Mardana did as Guru Nanak instructed, but came back again empty handed, and the people started to lose hope. Guru Nanak told them not to lose hope and sent Mardana yet again to Kandhari, promising that if he was refused a third time they would find another solution.

Mardana climbed the hill a third time and again asked for water with politeness but Kandhari was even more stubborn than before. He again repeated that if he has no money then he cannot use the water. A disappointed Mardana came back and fell, exhausted, in front of Guru Nanak. Guru Nanak took a stick and dug a small hole in the ground. Instantly, a spring of fresh water sprung up from the hole. The people were overjoyed at the sight. As they watched the water come before them, they quickly went to work to collect the water.

Wali Kandhari was watching all of this from the top of the hill. He could not believe his eyes, he then noticed that the water from his spring was drying up. He became furious.

In a fit of rage, he rolled a huge boulder over the hill in an attempt to kill Guru Nanak. Guru Nanak was sitting with his eyes closed, meditating calmly. People noticed the boulder coming their way and ran away, begging Guru Nanak to get out of the path of the boulder. But Guru Nanak would not move. He simply raised his hand to stop the boulder.

Guru Nanak's hand left its imprint on the boulder and it still can be seen today with the imprint of Guru's hand on it.

Realizing his mistake, Kandhari ran to Guru Nanak and begged for forgiveness. He was a changed man now and promised to live his life in a good way. He even allowed people to use water from his spring without having to pay for it, realizing that creations of God are meant to be shared by everyone.

The rock with the handprint of Guru Nanak can still be seen today at Panja Sahib in Pakistan. Guru Nanak forgave Kandhari, and all the people of the town were happy.

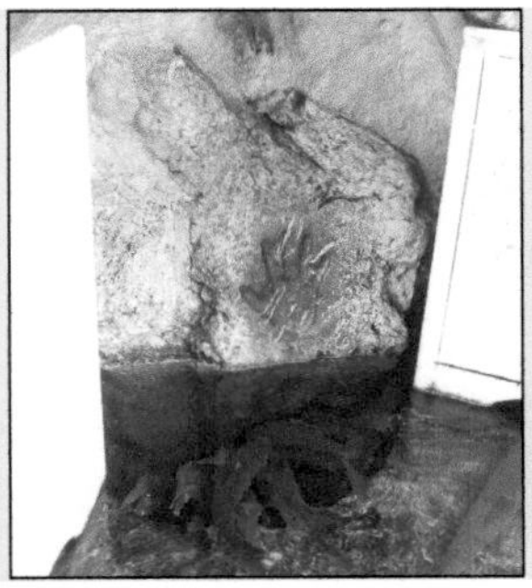

Gurdwara Panja Sahib Sarovar

The spring Guru Nanak opened continues to provide pure water which flows from a natural fountain beneath the boulder where his hand print is embedded. Despite attempts to remove it, the guru's handprint adorns the boulder to this day and can still be seen at the Sarovar of Gurdwara (temple) Panja Sahib in Pakistan.

The Story of Guru Nanak And Brahmins Throwing Water Towards The Sun

One day Guru Nanak saw some Brahmins (members of a priestly caste) standing in a river, scooping up water with their hands and throwing it towards the morning sun. Guru Nanak followed these Brahmins and started throwing water as well, but in the opposite direction.

Brahmin: "Stop. Stop", what are you doing?

Guru Nanak: "First, you tell me what are you doing?

Brahmin: "The Sun God is our ancestor, and we are thanking him for giving us blessings for prosperity and happiness. Now you tell us what you are doing?

Guru Nanak: I have a farm in the Punjab which is in this direction. My fields really need water in this summer season. If I don't get this water over to them, my crops might dry up.

Brahmin: How will water reach your farm from here?

Guru Nanak: Well, my farm is much closer than your ancestors. After a long discussion between the Brahmins, they asked "What should we do?"

Guru Nanak: Sincerely chant Sat Nam (God's name) and let it fill you with love. Pray from your heart. Be full of God every day and every moment. He advised them to help people, be with them and guide them to the Truth.

Shri Mataji On Guru Nanak

"Guru Nanaka always talked of Sahaja Yoga. About religion he said that observing fasts, going on pilgrimage, etc., are just meant to show off. Now you have to discover the power that is within you and establish it. Guru Nanak kept on repeating the same thing again and again. He never talked of rituals.

But when Guru Teg-Bahadur came, war with Mohammedan rulers was being fought. So he prescribed Kada (iron bangle), sword (kripan) to keep them in the state of preparedness. But Guru Nanaka always talked of the Spirit. He explained it very clearly, but no one heeded what he wrote. They will just put a finger on the couplet and read it out. Could we understand him this way? If we go through his writings properly and absorb it, then the whole shabad-jalam (confusion), in which most of the people are caught, will come to an end. Guru Nanaka said that I am prophet of Mohammedans and Guru of Hindus. Until one is realized one cannot understand this. "[44]

Talk Of Formless

"Nanak Sahib, according to His time, He said that you talk only of Formless. Talk of honey, talk of nectar, forget the flowers... Shri Guru Nanak has done such a wonderful work that he summarized the work of all the Self-Realized gurus and made the holy Granth Sahib (central religious scripture of Sikhism). If you wish to bow down, then bow down in front of Granth Sahib, which means you are bowing down in front of the consciousness (chai-tanya). Shri Mohammed Sahib also said the same thing, that do not bow down in front of anyone..."[45]

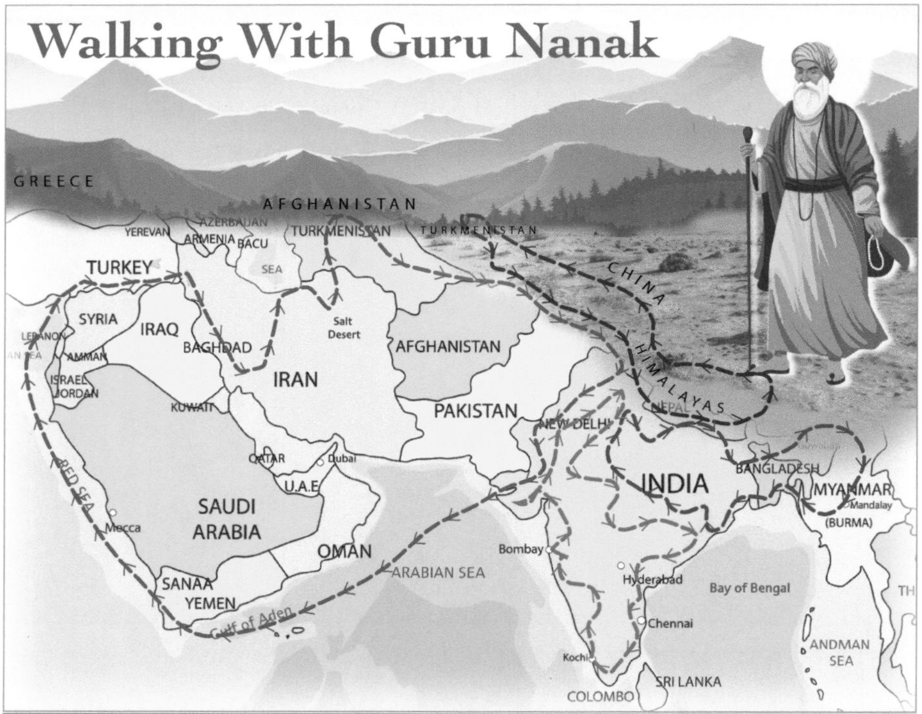

Guru Nanak and Mardana (Guru Nanak's close friend), traveled far and wide spreading the holy message of peace and compassion to all of mankind. Even though there are no exact accounts of his travels, he is believed to have made at least four major journeys, spanning more than 18,000 miles during a twenty-four year period.

Guru Nanak And Mecca

"Muhammad Sahib and Guru Nanak are the same personalities." He said, "How do You say that?" I said, "It is said that once Guru Nanaka was lying down and people said that, 'Sir, your feet are towards Mecca.' So, He said, 'All right I'll turn this side.' He turned on the other side and Mecca was on the other side. What does that mean?

"God has made everything and God sees everyone as equals."

-Guru Nanak

That means that Mecca is at the feet of Muhammad Sahib, also at the feet of Shri Guru Nanak. That means both of them are the same personalities."[46]

Even kings and emperors with heaps of wealth and vast dominion cannot compare with an ant filled with the love of God.

- Guru Nanak

Get Your Samadhi

"What Nanak Sahib has said, "Sahaja samadhi, now Sahaja samadhi." You have to get your samadhi; you have to become your Spirit. The time has come for that. There is no need to have so many religions. All religions are respected within yourself because they all reside within you. You do not know how important every religion is to us, is extremely important. We do not know the essence of all the religions, we are just outside, that's why. So the child should be called a Sahaja yogi who is "dharmateet" (beyond dharma)," who is "gunateet (beyond the gunas or energy channels)", who is "kalateet (beyond time)."[47]

Granth Sahib

"So you must only bow your heads before an authorized guru. It is alright if you go to the Gurudwara and bow before the Granth Sahib (Holy Book). Because Granth Sahib is the truth. When there is already the Granth Sahib, there is no other guru worthy of bowing to. So only bow to the Granth Sahib."[48]

Questions & Answers

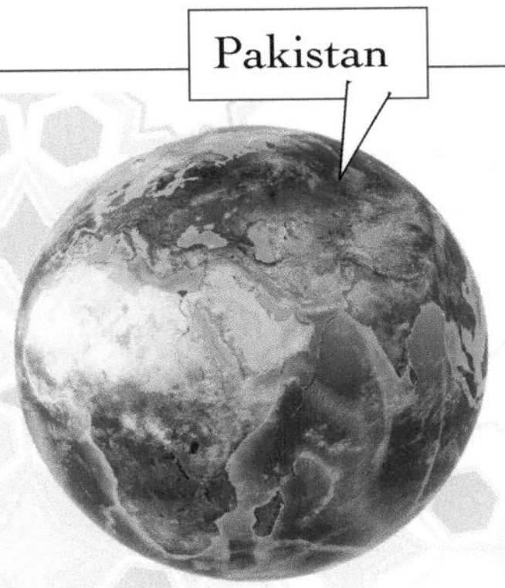

For how many days did Guru Nanak disappear under the water in the river?

- Guru Nanak disappeared for two days and reappeared on the morning of the third day.

How many years did Guru Nanak spend travelling and how many miles did he travel?

- Guru Nanak spent 24 years travelling spreading his message of peace. He travelled more then 18,000 miles.

What was the main message of Guru Nanak?

- Guru Nanak's main message was that everyone is equal, regardless of how one looks or how much money one has. God loves equally all girls and boys as well as old and young people.

Shri Mataji had said that Guru Nanak and another primordial master are the same person. Which primordial master did Shri Mataji talk about?

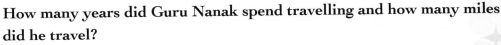

- Shri Mataji said that Guru Nanak and Muhammad Sahib are the same person.

Sainath of Shirdi

Shirdi Sai Baba, also called Sai Baba of Shirdi, was a spiritual leader dear to Hindu and Muslim devotees throughout India. The name Sai Baba of Shirdi comes from 'Sai', a Persian word used by Muslims to denote a holy person, and 'Baba', a Hindi word for father. Shirdhi refers to the village where he lived.

Sai Baba's early years are a mystery. Sai Baba arrived in Shirdi village in 1858. Shirdi village is located in the Western state of Maharastra, India, where he lived until his death in 1918.

Baba lived under a neem tree in Shirdhi and often wandered around in the jungle for long periods of time. His manner was said to have been withdrawn and uncommunicative as he sat for long periods in meditation.

The villagers were awestruck to see such a young man submerged in hard penance, not bothered by heat or cold. During the day, he spoke to no one, in the night, he was not afraid of anybody. His presence attracted the curiosity of a few people drawn to his religious practice, while others such as the village children considered him mad and threw stones at him. At first, he was denounced by the villagers of Shirdi as a madman, but by the turn of the century, Sai Baba had a considerable following of Hindus and Muslims. His followers were attracted by his compelling teachings and his performance of apparent miracles. He also gave 'dharshan' (appearance of a holy person/deity) to people in the form of Sri Rama, Shri Krishna, Shri Vithala, Shri Shiva and many other Gods depending on the faith of the devotees. According to them, Sai Baba appeared

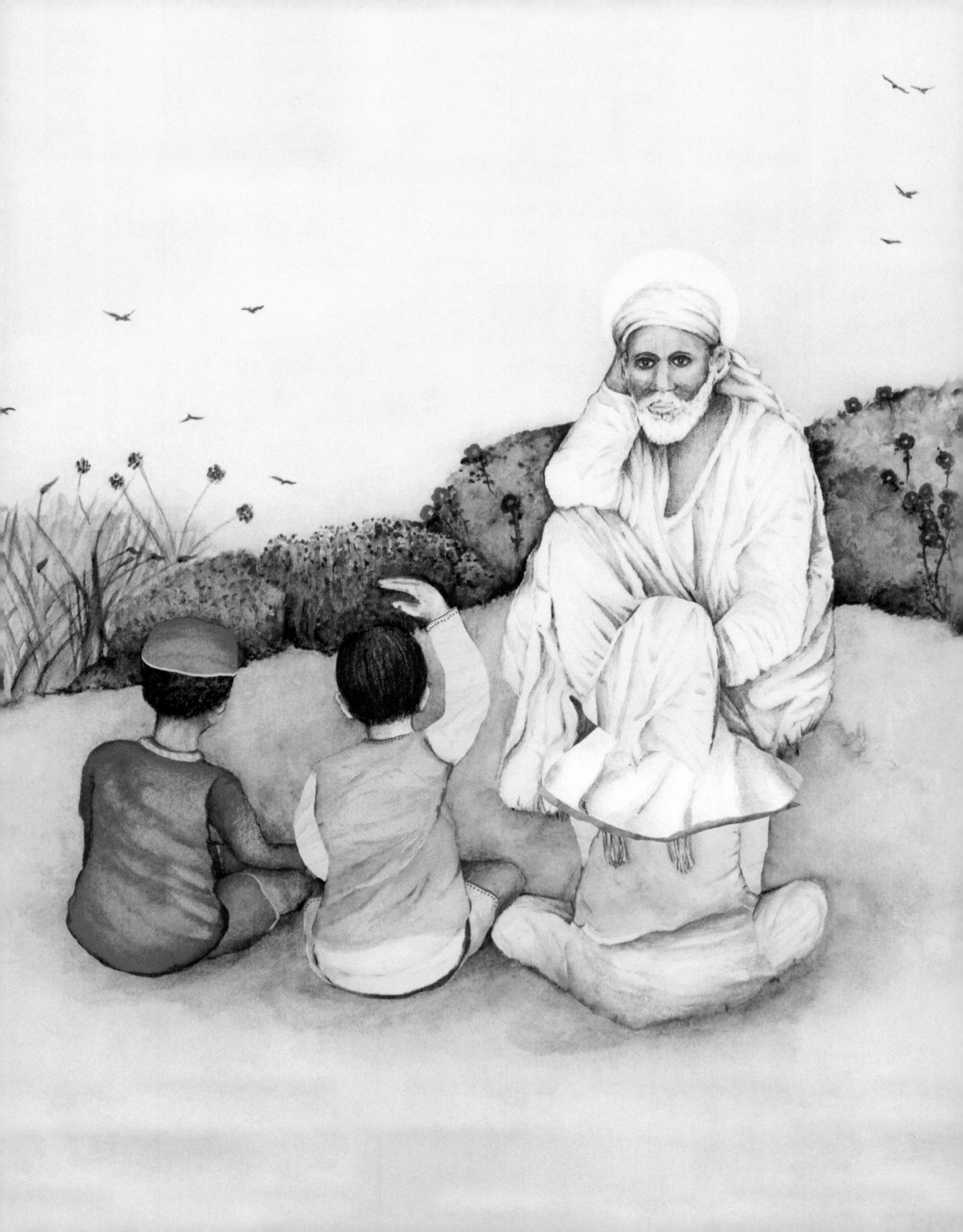

Sai Baba Performs Miracles

- Turning water into oil
- Stopping the rain
- Levitation (being afloat in the air)
- Bilocation (ability of an individual or object to be in two places at the same time)
- Reading people's minds
- Removal of body parts and fixing them
- Saving people by stopping a falling mosque ceiling
- Curing the sick

First Photos Of Sai Baba

A British officer took original photos of Shirdhi Sai Baba. In reality, he wanted to take pictures of Sai Baba to submit to the English court stating that Baba was cheating people of Shirdi. When he developed the pictures he took of Sai Baba, without his permission, he found Lord Jesus Christ in it instead of Sai Baba. He realized that Baba was not an ordinary man, and he apologized for his mistake. Then he asked him for a picture, and this time, the photo showed the image of Shri Sai Baba in it.

Turning Water Into Oil Miracle

Every night, Sai Baba used to light the lamps in the Dwarkamai (name of the mosque where Sai Baba lived in Shirdi). He asked various store owners to give him oil for free. In the beginning, the storekeepers looked down upon Baba calling him a mad 'fakir' (a Muslim religious ascetic who lives solely on alms) and the grocers gave him oil merely to make fun of him. But soon they got fed up with this daily practice, and one day, they all refused to give him oil. With the empty oil-tin dangling from his hand, Baba came back to Dwarkamai. He put a little water in the oil can and drank it to please the God within. Then he took more water, poured it in the lamps and kindled them, one by one. Soon, the 'water-lamps' burned throughout the mosque.

Story Of Wheat Berry Grinding Miracle

One time, there was an epidemic of cholera in Shirdi. The helpless Shirdi people approached Baba. To help the villagers Baba washed his hands and face and took some wheat berries and started grinding them in a hand mill. Then he asked the village people to take the flour and spread it along the village borders. To the villager's delight, from that time onward the cholera epidemic subsided, and the people of the village were safe and happy. By grinding wheat berries Baba symbolically ground the chlorella itself and pushed it out of the village.

to them in their dreams and gave them advice. His devotees have documented many stories of these events.

Baba was completely opposed to orthodoxy, Hinduism, Christianity and Islam. Instead, he asked his devotees to lead an ordinary life. He followed all Hindu rituals and permitted Muslims to follow Namaz (Islamic prayer). Shri Sai Baba wanted to belong to all and be part of all. When pressed on whether he was a Hindu or a Muslim, he would often get very angry.

Baba had been persuaded to take up residence in Dwarkamai, an old mosque. There he lived a solitary life. He lived off begging for alms from Hindu or Muslim visitors. In his mosque, he maintained a sacred fire which is referred to as a 'dhuni' (sacred fire). Baba gave sacred ash ('udi') to his guests from this dhuni. Its ashes were believed to have healing powers.

In August 1918, Shirdi Sai Baba told some of his devotees that he would soon be "leaving his mortal body" (dying). Towards the end of September, he had high fever and stopped eating. On October 15, 1918, he took his last breath. He took 'samadhi' (he passed away).

Sainath of Shirdi original photo in 1916.

When Sainath found that so many people were smoking this tobacco, he smoked all the tobacco of the world. He tried to smoke everything in Maharashtra so that nobody should get it. That Is the style of Shiva, to take all the poison into Himself.

He advised his devotees and followers to lead a moral life, help others, love every living being without any discrimination, and develop two important qualities of character: faith ('shraddha') and patience ('saburi').

Sai Baba left behind no spiritual heirs, appointed no disciples, and did not provide formal initiation ('diksha'), despite many requests from his followers. Sai Baba's main message was of love, helping people, charity, universal brotherhood, contentment, forgiveness, living a detached life as well as devotion to one's guru. He lived an ascetic life (the purpose of pursuing spiritual goals) and helped everyone who came to him, and he asked his followers and disciples to live the life of a householder without any attachments to worldly things.

Baba's Words On Charity

- Shri Sai Baba encouraged charity and stressed the importance of sharing.
- If any creature comes to you for help, don't drive them away. Receive them with respect and treat them well.
- Give water to the thirsty, food to the hungry, and allow a stranger to take accommodation on your verandah.
- If someone asked you for money, and you are not inclined to give any, don't give, but don't bark at him unnecessarily.
- Baba always said, "Love every living being without any discrimination".

Shri Mataji On Sainath Of Shirdi

"Shirdhi Sainath ... was a Muslim, but in Maharashtra he is respected as a big saint.... He (a British officer) took a photograph of Sai Baba, all his folds

Interesting Facts

- Everyone is equal. Shri Shirdi Sai Baba followed both, Islam and Hinduism. He went to the mosque as well as to the temples. He use to sing about Allah in a Hindu temple and praised Shri Rama and Shri Shiva in a mosque.

- Sai Baba's disciples and devotees claimed that he has performed many miracles.Sai Baba has helped people to overcome many distresses. Those were all miracles and his blessings, but he never showed off his powers.

- Baba preached to his devotees to keep faith in God and to obtain their self-realization. He did not want people to become materialistic.

- Sai Baba lived under a neem tree for five years and used to wander into the forest in Shirdi.

were there, and on the fold my face came, completely, with my round thing, and face, eyes, everything. The complete face came on it. So the sheeshya showed him, the one who had taken the photograph. He said, "Who is this?" He said, "This is my Mother. And She's going to come back one day." Now, this one, this photograph was then acquired by his son. And he saw my photograph.... This fellow, when he saw my photograph, he came to me and he said that, "See, Mother your photograph was in Saint's clothes and all that. We wrote to him this thing, that and we got a book also. And this is your photo graph." I said, "It's true." "Were You his Mother?" I said, "It's true. I was his Mother."[49]

Sainath And Tobacco

"When Sai Nath found that so many people were smoking this tobacco, he smoked all the tobacco of the world. He tried to smoke everything in Maharashtra so that nobody should get it. That is the style of Shiva, to take all the poison into Himself. " Sainath was against all the rituals and conditioning because these are misleading. After awakening, things change, of course. Realized people become knowledgeable. Without Realization, it is not possible. So Sai Nath did not organize. We have not organized too. We have no organization. People automatically get organized after awakening, the way different organs of the body are organized. So without any organization, everything is going on immaculately in Sahaja Yoga."[50]

Love Personified

"The left-hand side is the emotional feeling about things. You feel tremendous love for others.... Sai Nath was one of them who had this left-hand side gift with him and he was love personified. And he was so much full of love for people that once there was a woman who was very poor, and she could not celebrate Diwali, and he could not bear it, so he gave her some water, and the water became like oil, and she burnt lights in that. And it is a fact. You can do that. It is possible."[51]

> "It is essential to practice spiritual disciplines along with academic studies."
>
> *- Sainath of Shirdhi*

> **"Sai Nath was one of them who had this left-hand side gift with him and he was love personified."**
>
> *-Shri Mataji Nirmala Devi*

Words Of Wisdom By Sainath Of Shirdhi

"Anger, ego, and jealousy are the biggest diseases. Keep yourself aloof from these three diseases."

"Gain and loss, birth and death are in the hands of God."

"Keep faith and patience and your prayer shall be answered."

"When times are hard and you wonder where God is, remember, teachers are always quiet during the test."

"There is only one caste, the caste of humanity. There is only one religion, the religion of love. There is only one language, the language of the heart."

"Love one another and help others to rise to the higher levels, simply by pouring out love. Love is infectious and the greatest healing energy."

"What matters is to live in the present, live now, for every moment is now. It is your thoughts and acts of the moment that create your future."

"The life ahead can only be glorious if you learn to live in total harmony with the Lord."

Questions & Answers

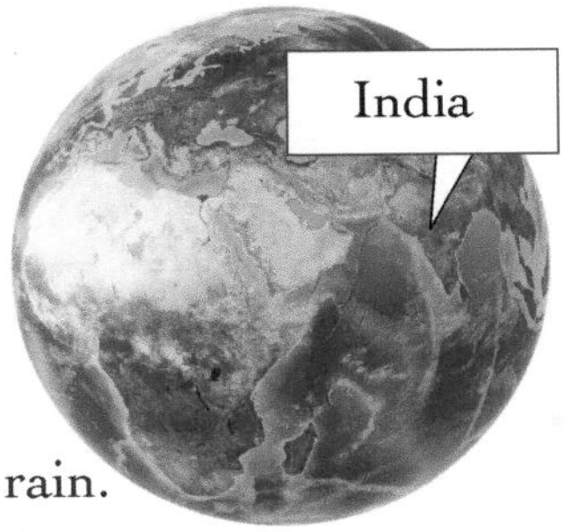

When and where was Sai Nath of Shirdhi born?
- He was born in India, 1838.

What are some miracles that Sai Nath of Shirdhi performed?
- Curing the sick, reading people's minds, levitation, bilocation, stopping the rain.

Why did a British officer take a picture of Sai Nath of Shirdhi?
- He wanted to take pictures of Sai Baba to submit to the English court stating, Baba is cheating people of Shirdi.

What was Sai Nath of Shirdhi's last wish for his devotees and followers?
- He wished his devotees and followers to lead a moral life, help others, love every living being without any discrimination, and develop two important qualities of character: faith and patience.

When Shri Mataji spoke about Sai Nath of Shirdhi, how did she describe him?
- Shri Mataji said that Sainath of Shirdhi was love personified and that he had so much of love for people.

MIRACLE

What liquid did Sai Nath of Shirdhi turn into oil?
- Water.

Endnotes

1 Shri Mataji Nirmala Devi, 29 November, 1982
2 - https://en.wikipedia.org
3 Shri Mataji Nirmala Devi, 10 September, 1983
4 Shri Mataji Nirmala Devi, 10 September, 1983
5 Shri Mataji Nirmala Devi, 3 April, 1981
6 Shri Mataji Nirmala Devi, 9 December, 1973
7 Shri Mataji Nirmala Devi, 20 December, 1988
8 - https://en.wikipedia.org
9 Shri Mataji Nirmala Devi, 19 August, 1990
10 Shri Mataji Nirmala Devi, 27 March, 1981
11 Shri Mataji Nirmala Devi, 25 March, 1982
12 Shri Mataji Nirmala Devi, 29 October, 1982
13 Shri Mataji Nirmala Devi, 29 October, 1982
14 Shri Mataji Nir,mala Devi, 23 November, 1980
15 Shri Mataji Nirmala Devi, 25 May, 1997
16 - https://en.wikipedia.org
17 Shri Mataji Nirmala Devi, 13 July, 1994
18 - https://en.wikipedia.org
19 Shri Mataji Nirmala Devi, Russia 1995
20 Shri Mataji Nirmala Devi, 9 October, 1986
21 Shri Mataji Nirmala Devi, 13 September, 1995
22 Shri Mataji Nirmala Devi, 13 September 1995
23 Shri Mataji Nirmala Devi, 20 March, 2001
24 Shri Mataji Nirmala Devi, 1 January, 1991
25 Shri Mataji Nirmala Devi, 10 March. 1996
26 Shri Mataji Nirmala Devi, 27 June, 1985
27 Shri Mataji Nirmala Devi, 9 September, 1995
28 - https://en.wikipedia.org/
29 - https://en.wikipedia.org
30 Shri Mataji Nirmala Devi, 25 May, 1985
31 - https://en.wikipedia.org
32 Shri Mataji Nirmala Devi, 24 May, 1989
33 Shri Mataji Nirmala Devi, 19 June, 2018
34 The Meta Modern Era, Shri Mataji Nirmala Devi
35 Shri Mataji Nirmala Devi, Talk in England, 1981
36 Shri Mataji Nirmala Devi, Talk in England 1981
37 Shri Mataji Nirmala Devi, 18 May, 1993
38 Shri Mataji Nirmaa Devi, 19 June, 1983
39 Shri Mataji Nirmala Devi, 31 March, 1983
40 Shri Mataji Nirmala Devi, 27 December, 1990
41 Shri Mataji Nirmala Devi, 10 September, 1993
42 Shri Mataji Nirmala Devi, 26 March, 1974
43 Shri Mataji Nirmala Devi, 7 March, 1981
44 Shri Mataji Nirmala Devi, 21 February, 1986
45 Shri Mataji Nirmala Devi, 21 February, 1986
46 Shri Mataji Nirmala Devi, 17 March, 1984
47 Shri Mataji Nirmala Devi, 17 March, 1984
48 Shri Mataji Nirmala Devi, 2 February, 1983
49 Shri Mataji NIrmala Devi, 28 May, 1985
50 Shri Mataji Nirmala Devi, 23 November, 1999
51 Shri Mataji Nirmala Devi, 26 January, 1977

CPSIA information can be obtained
at www.ICGtesting.com
Printed in the USA
LVHW071039190321
681922LV00013B/637